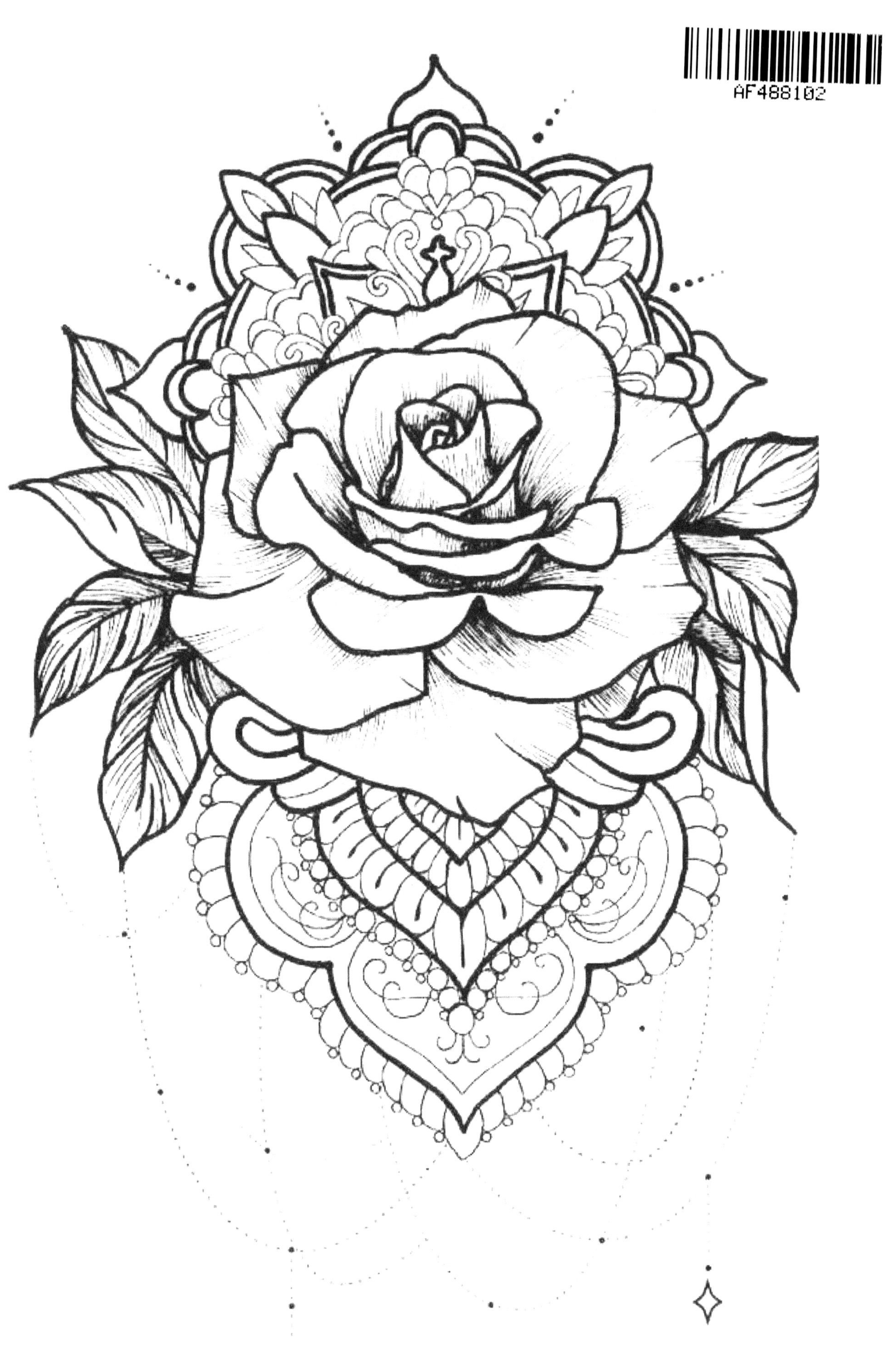

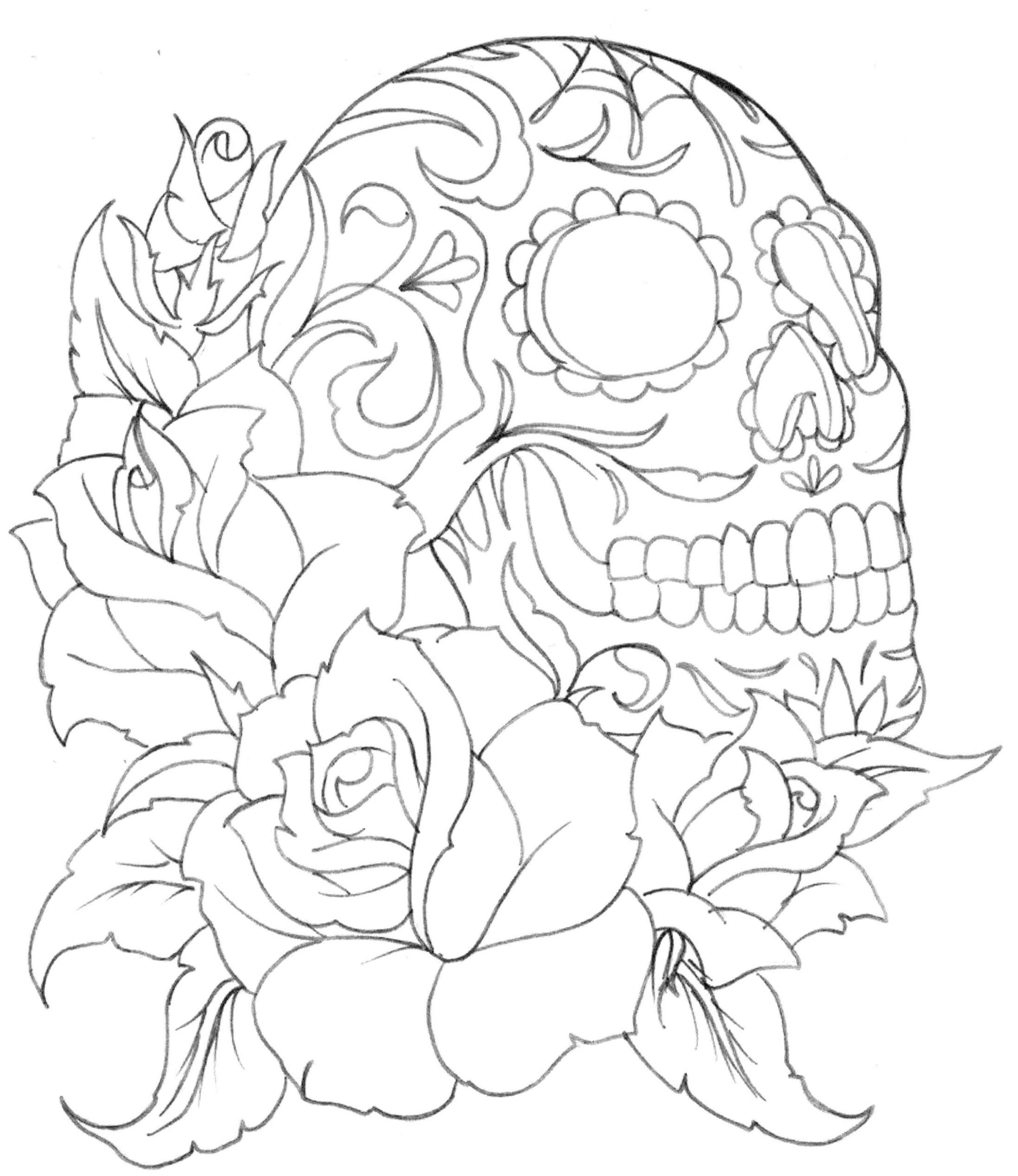

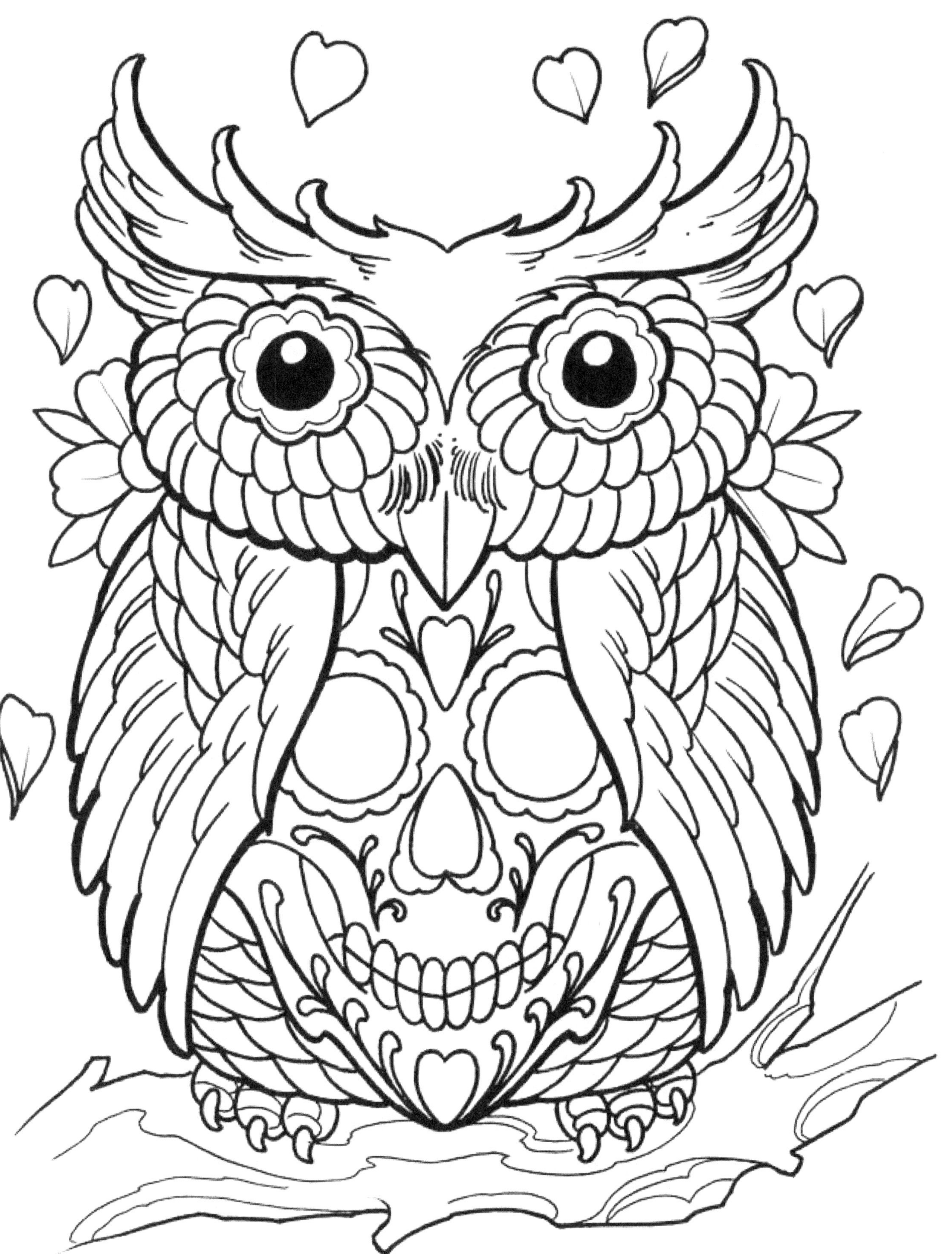

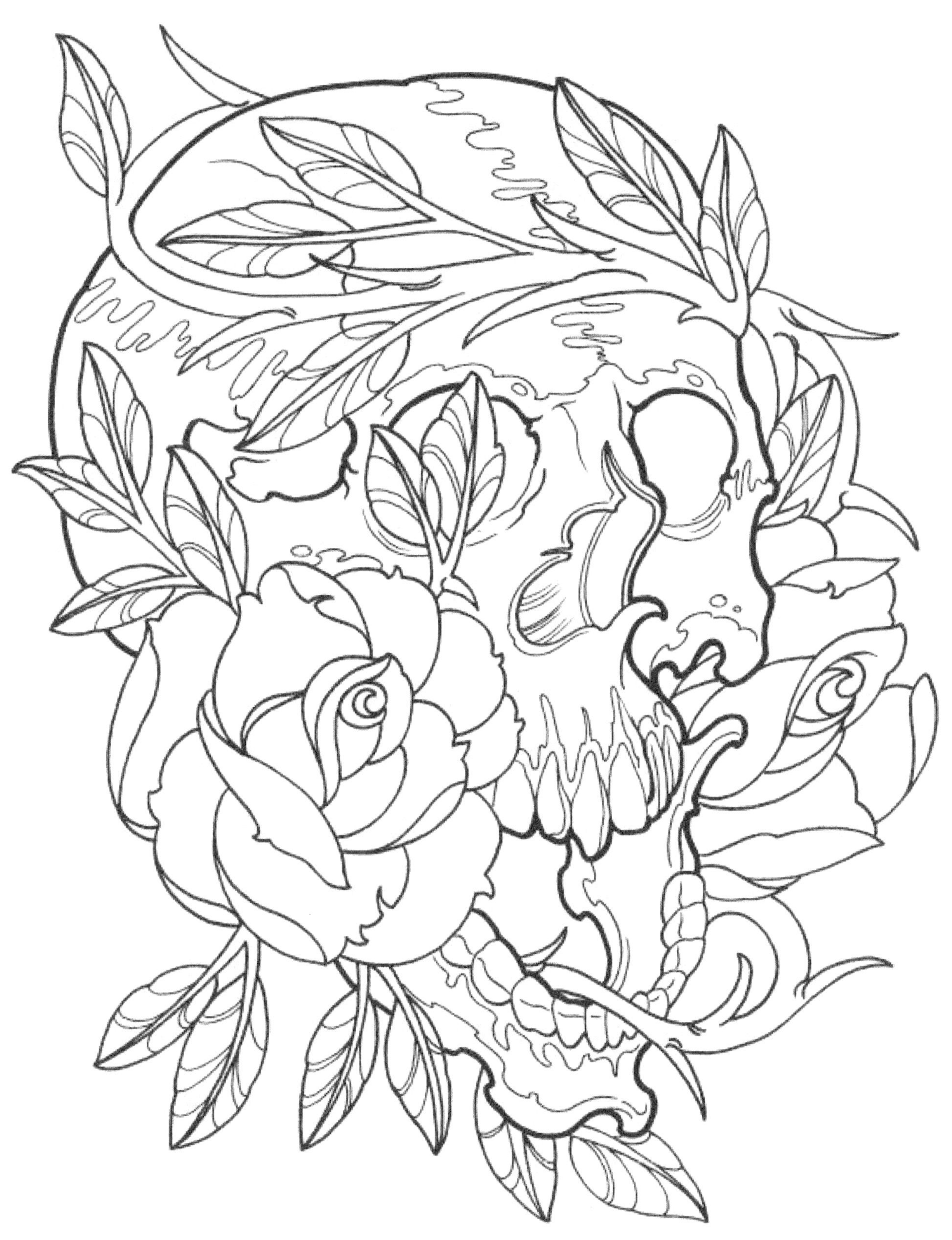

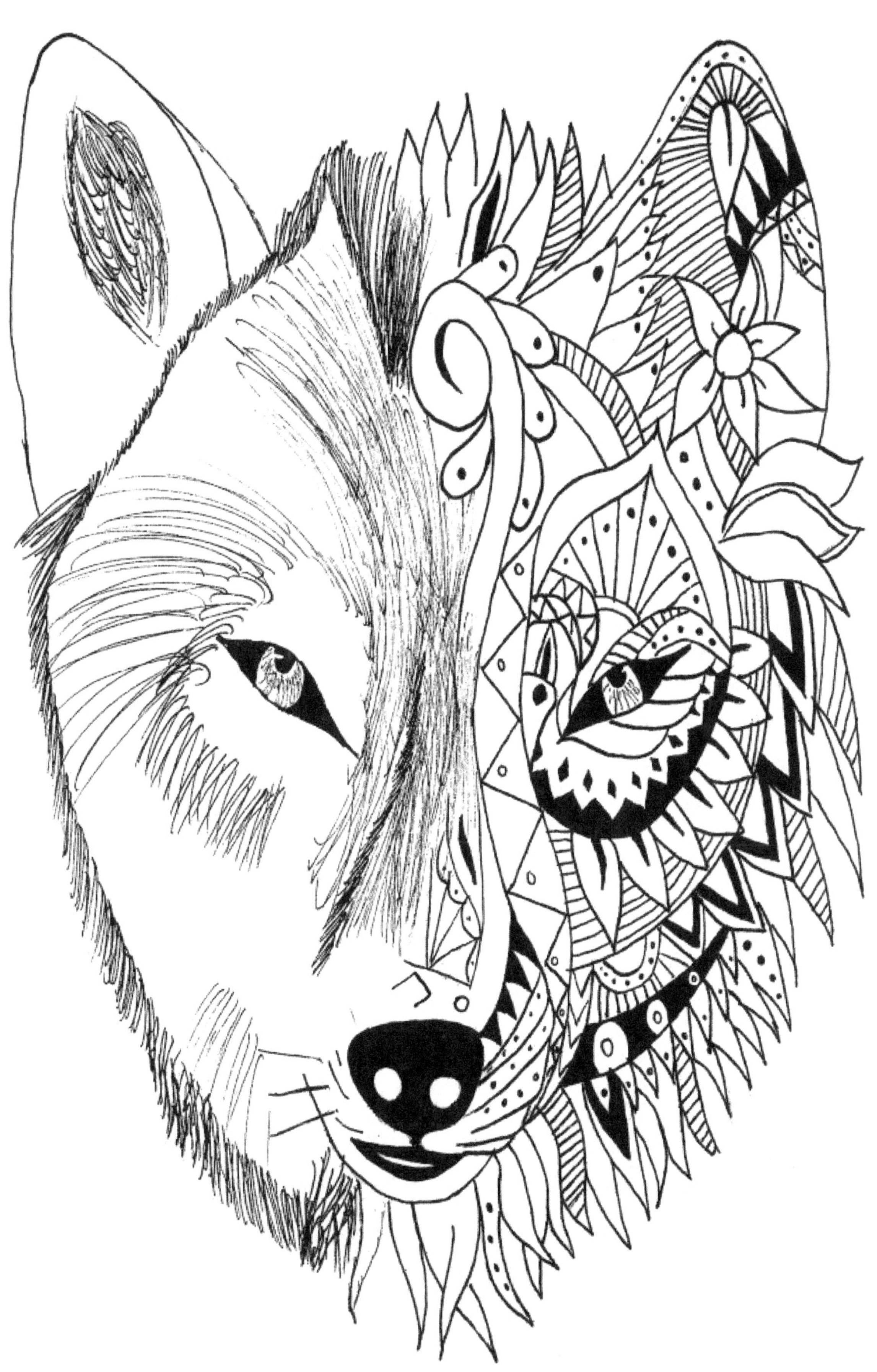

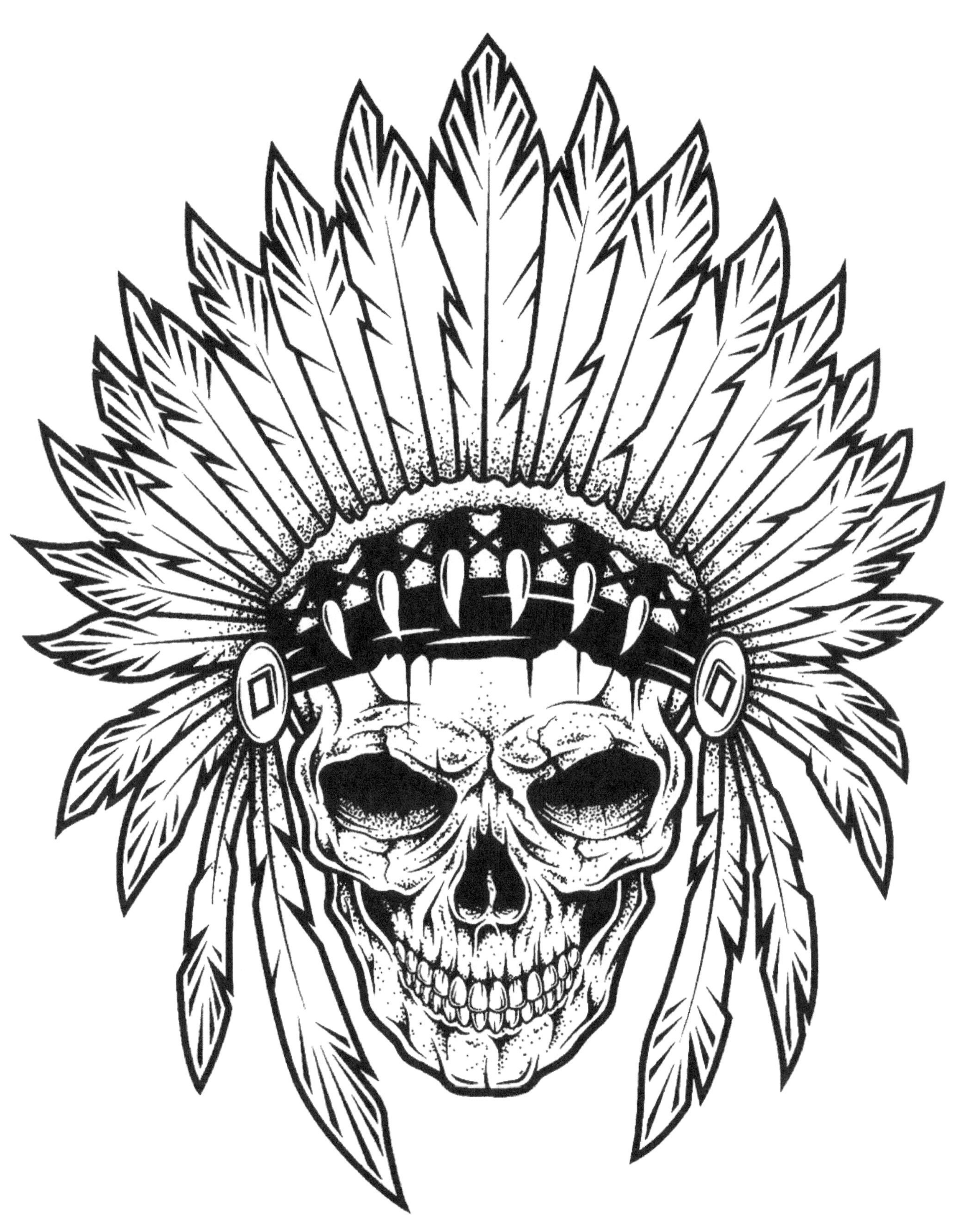

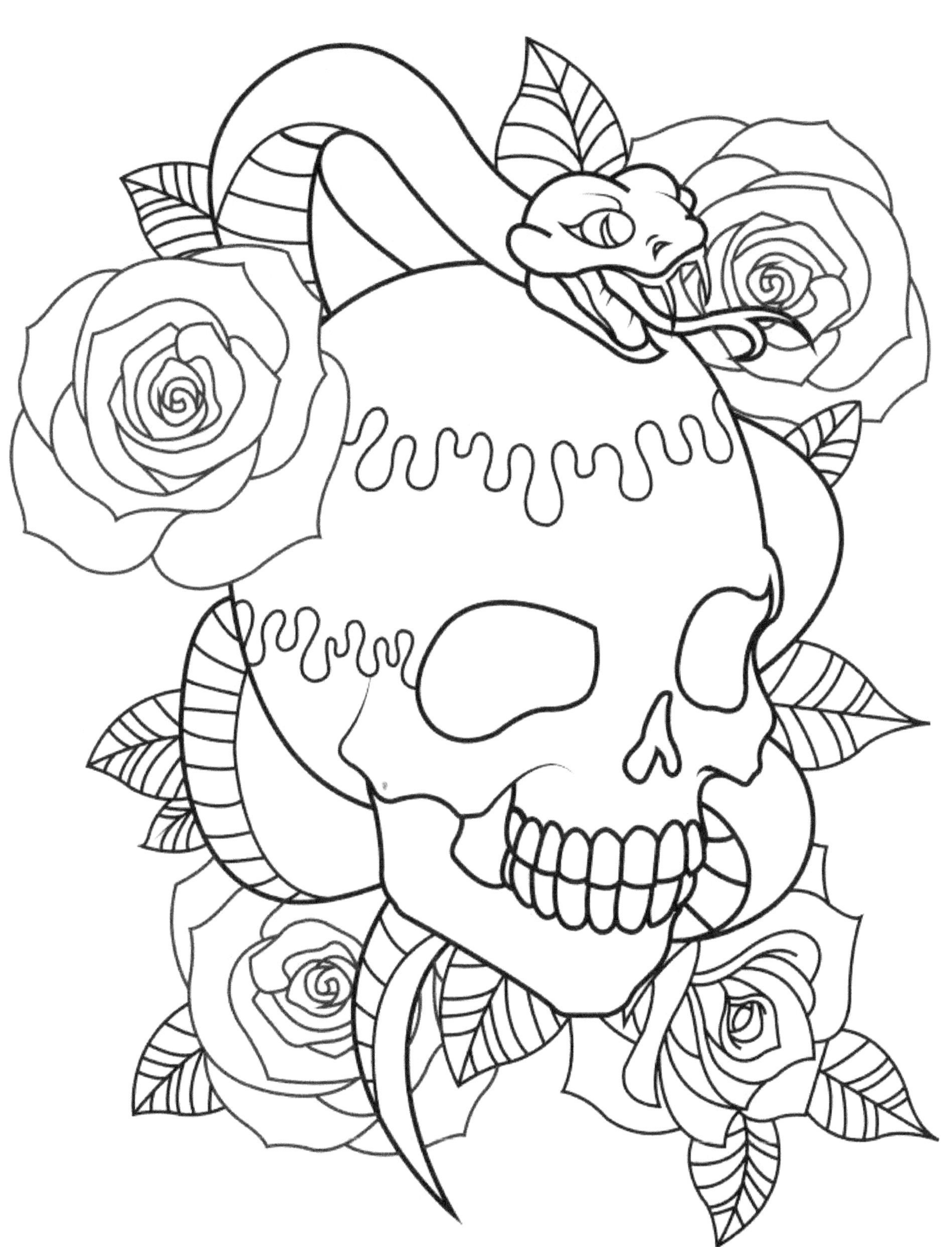

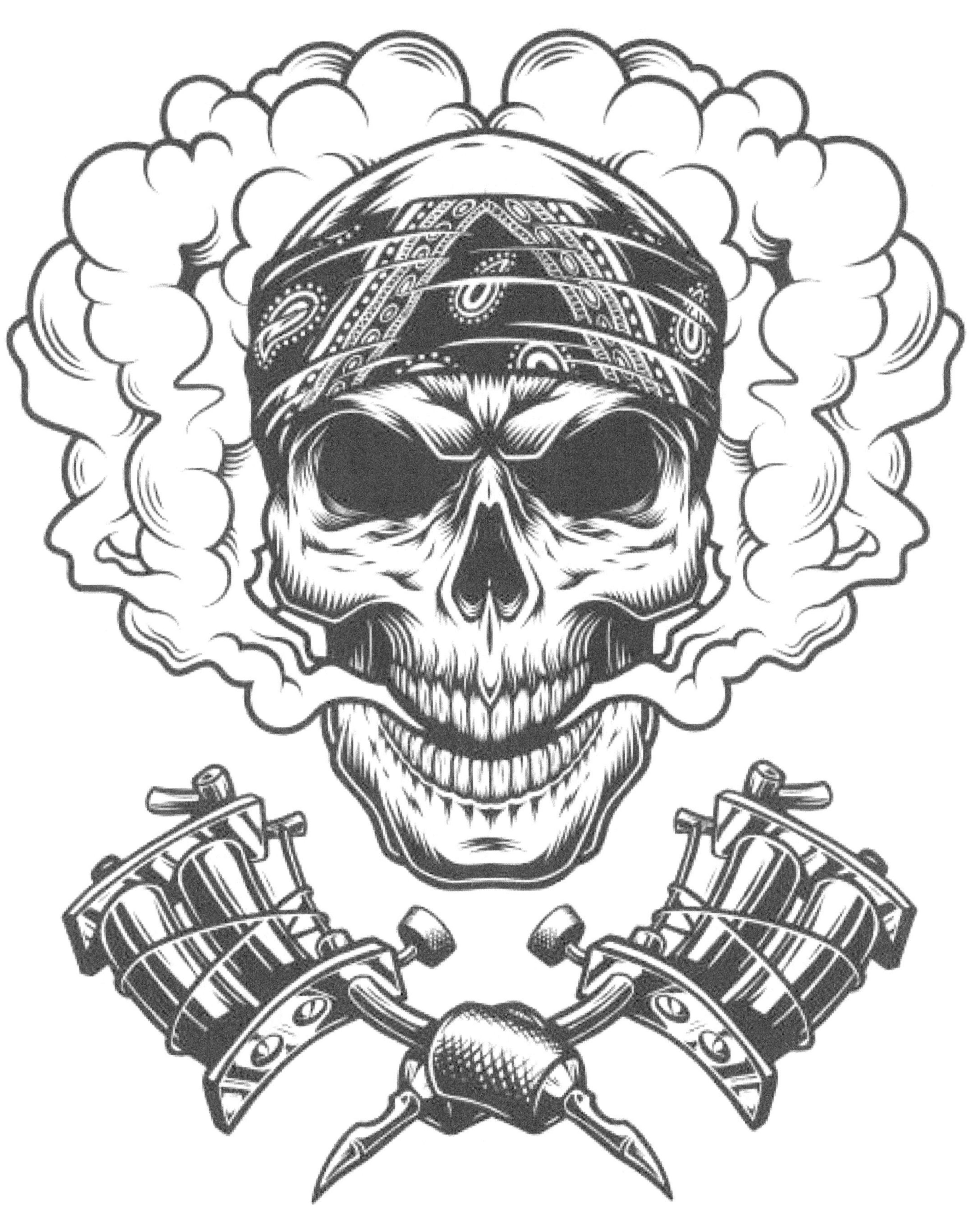

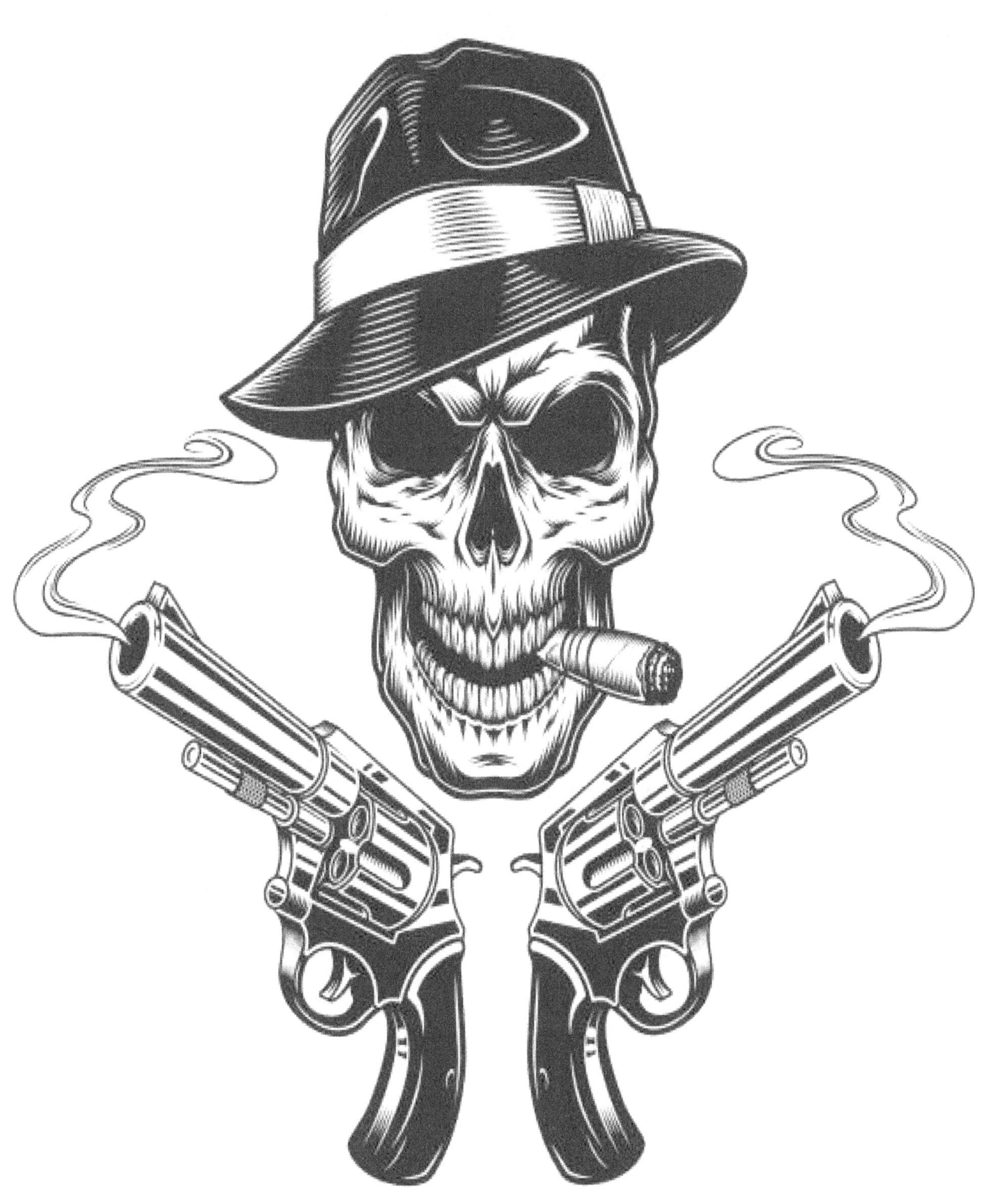

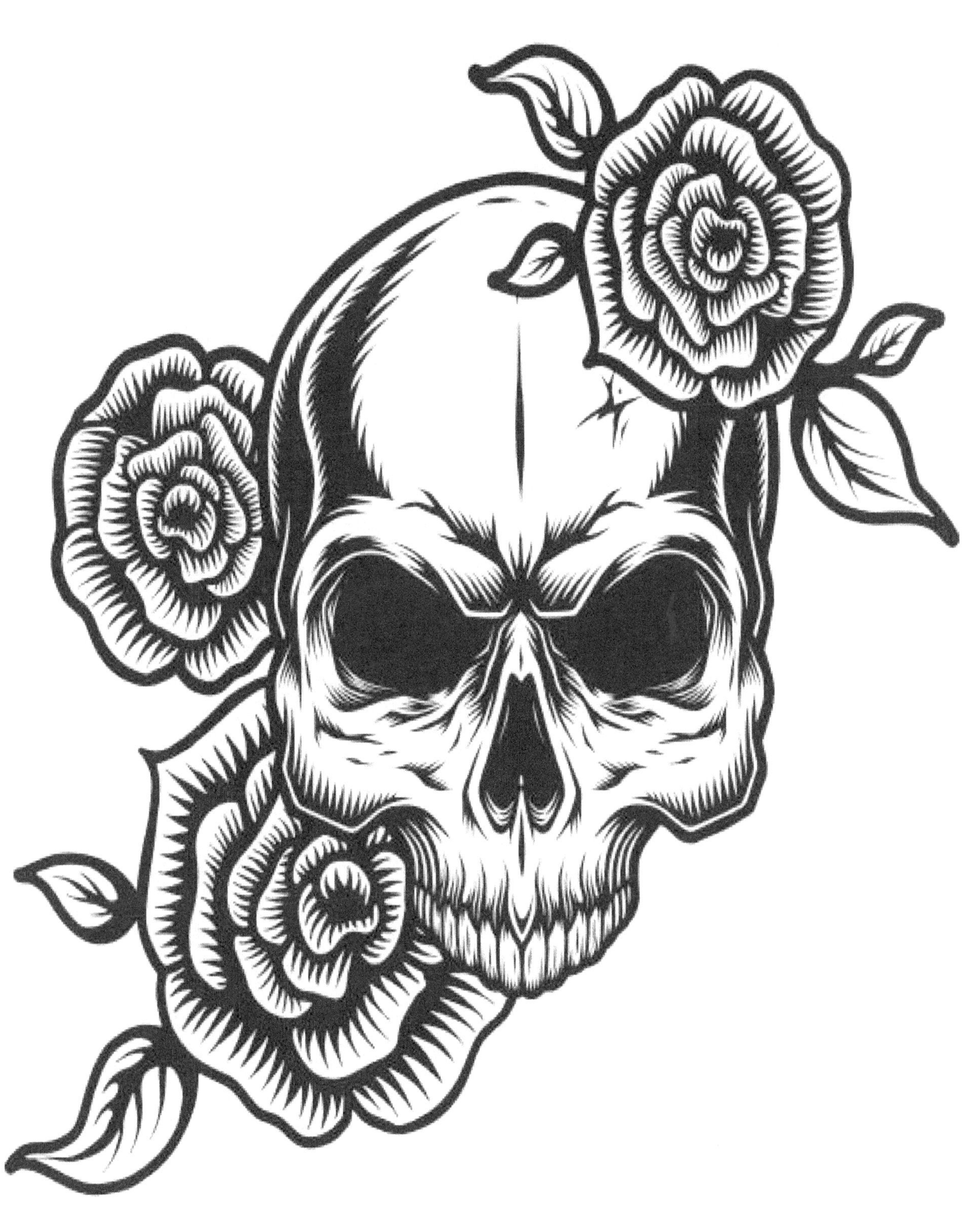

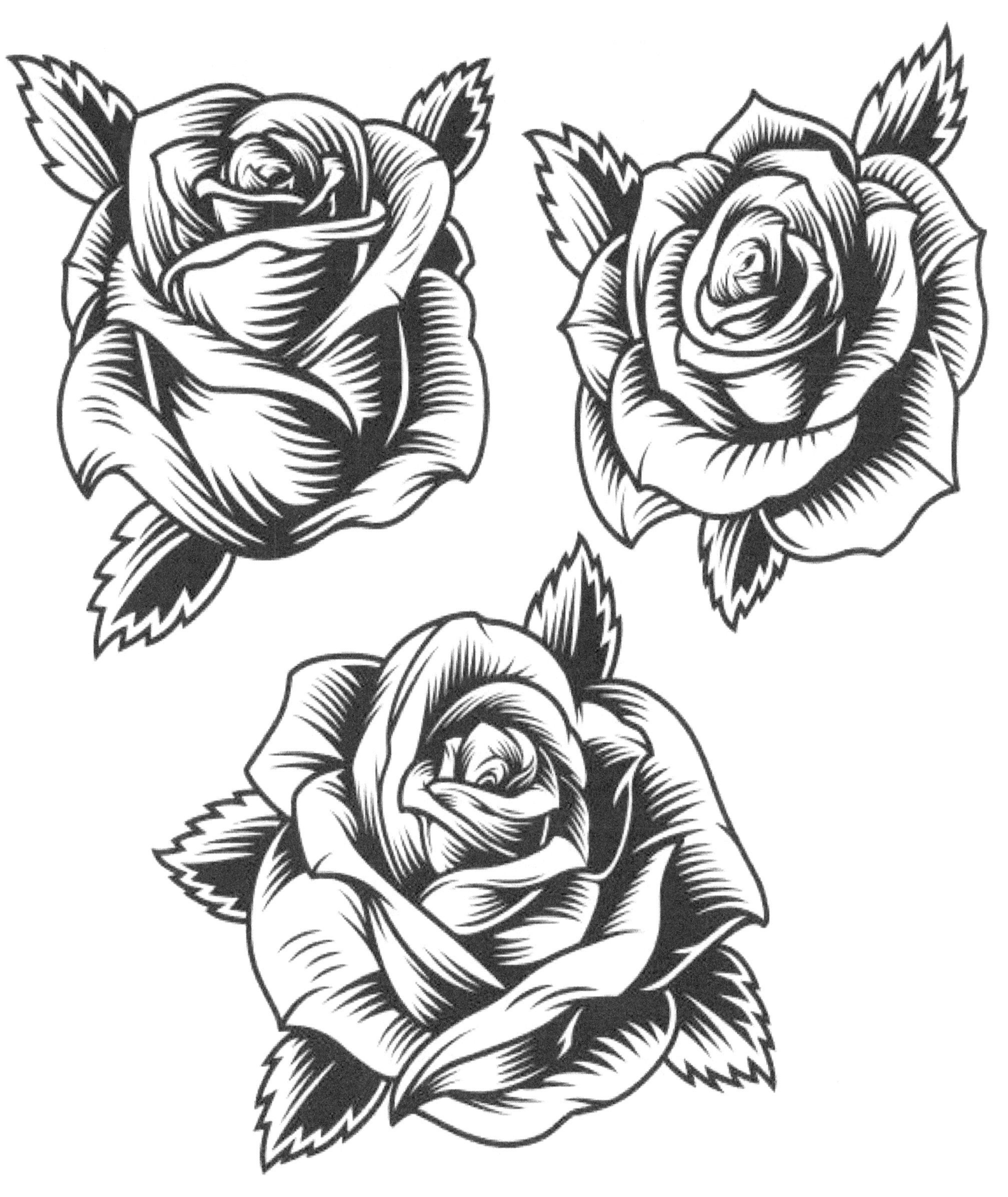

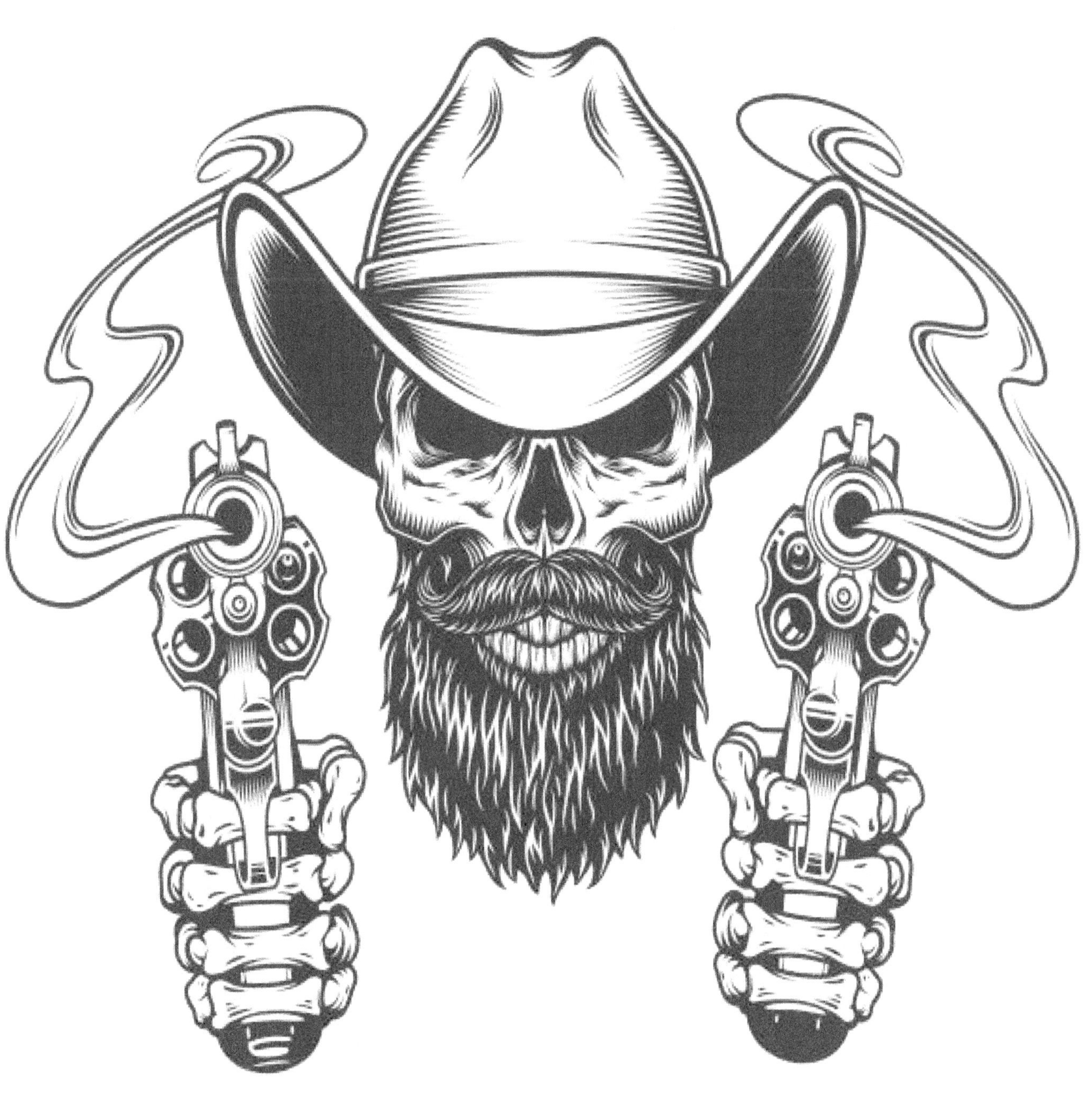

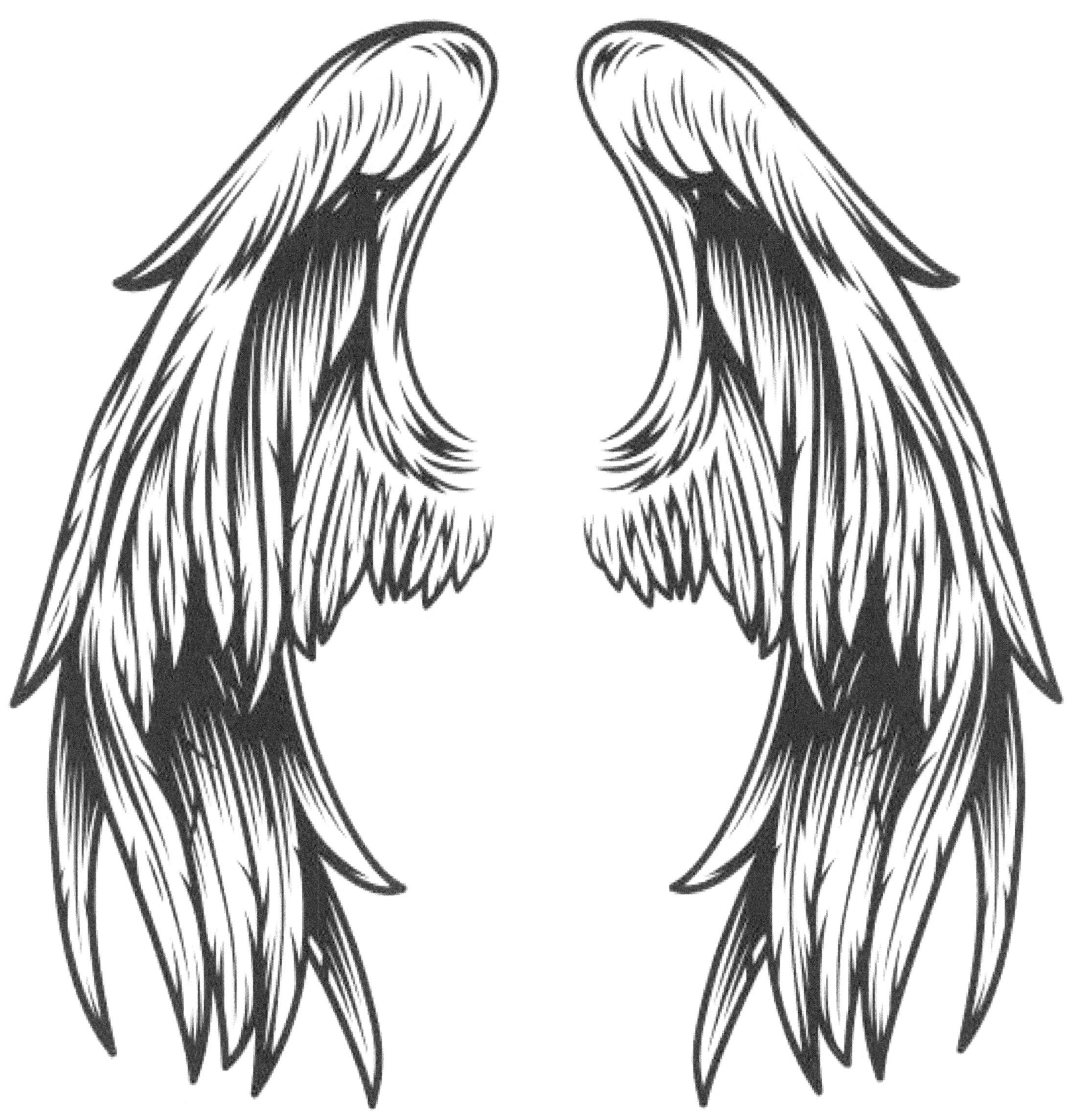

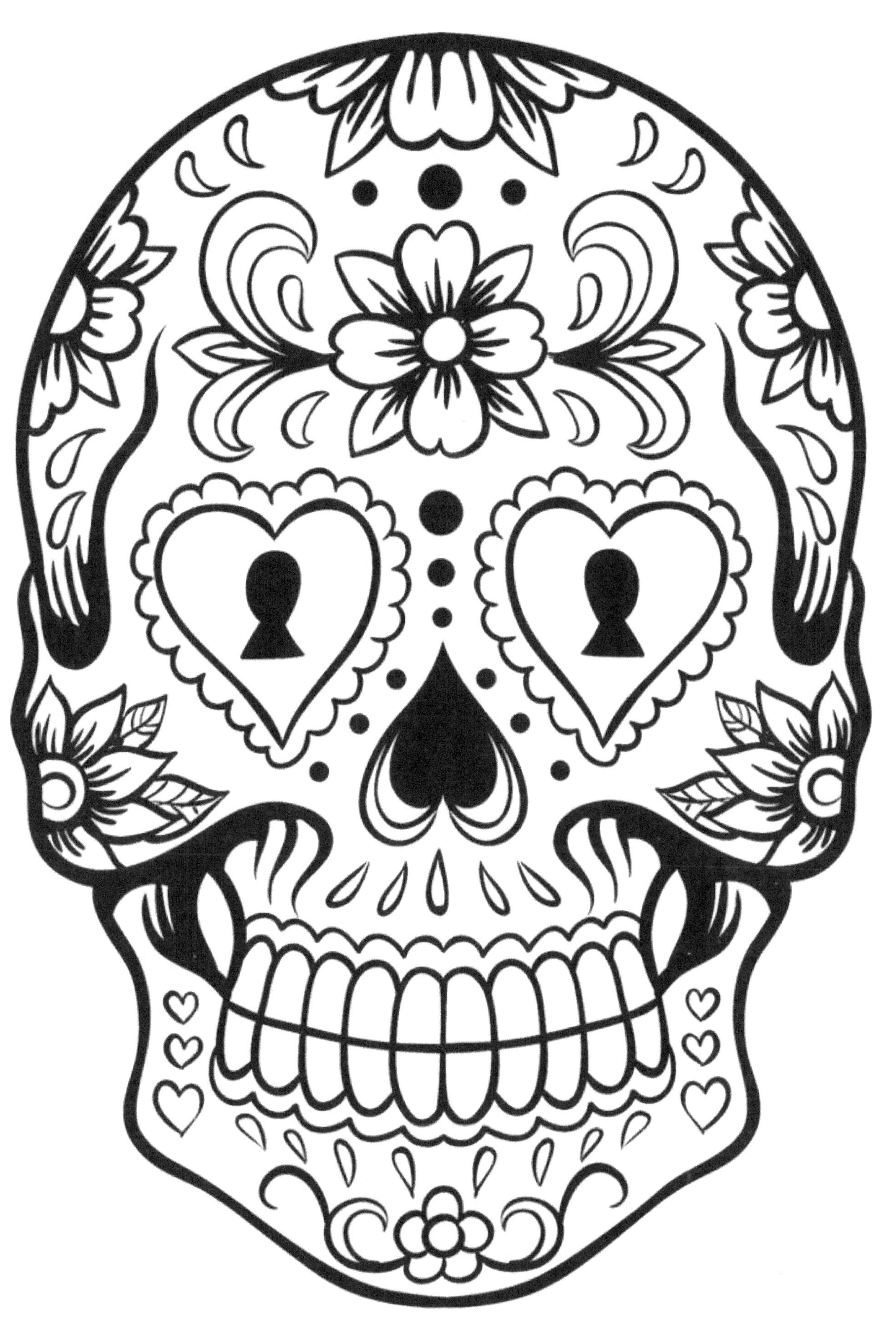

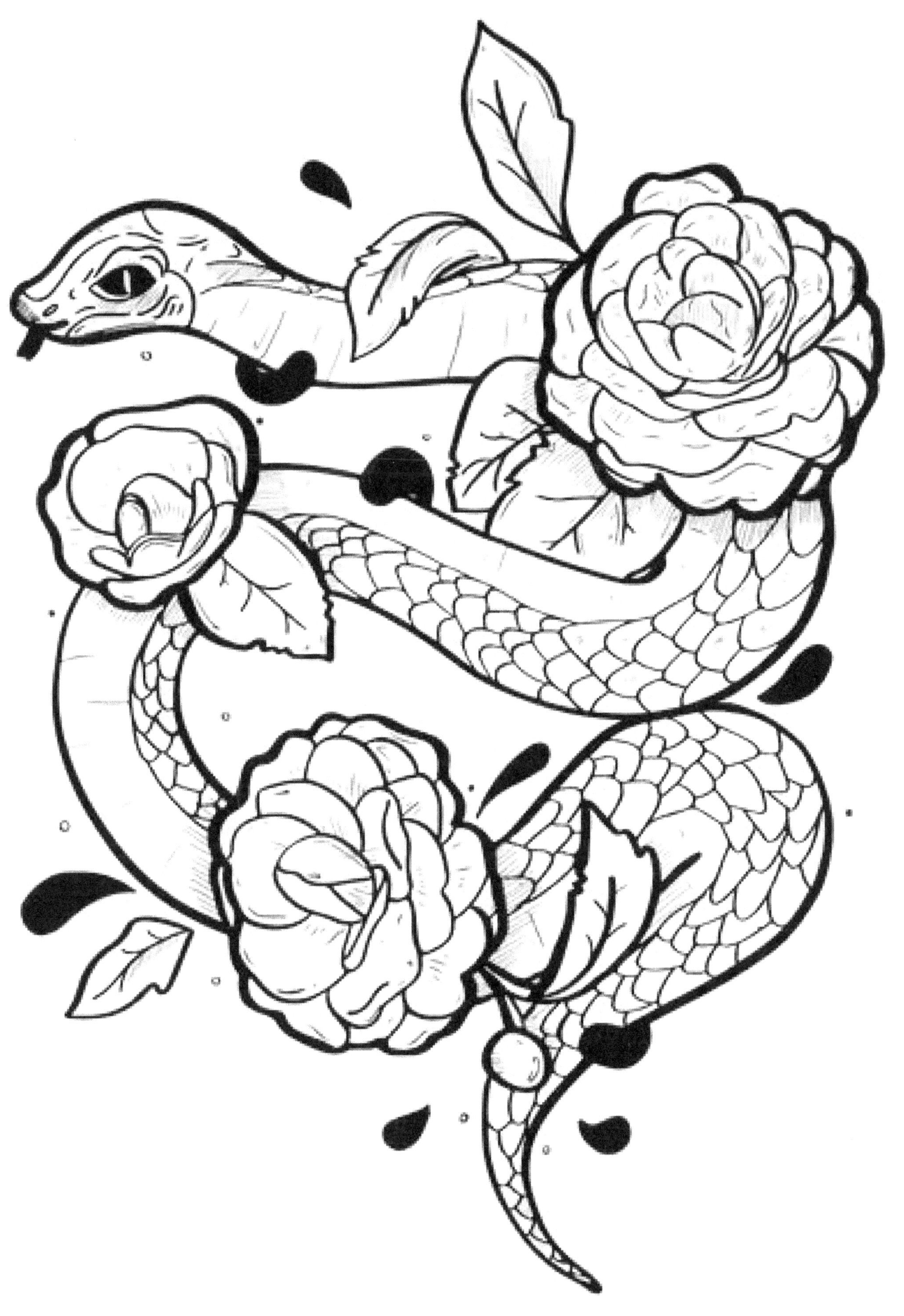

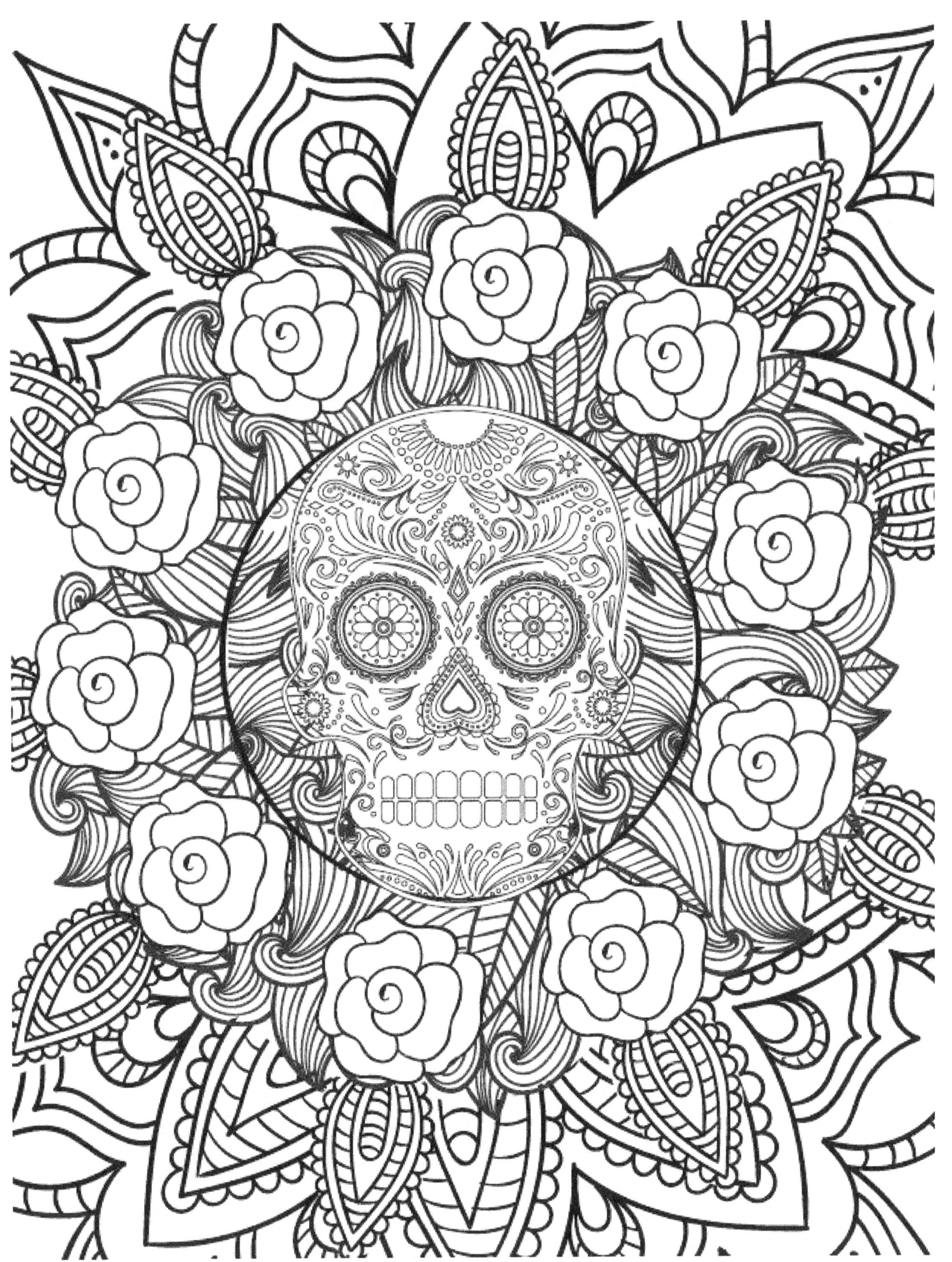

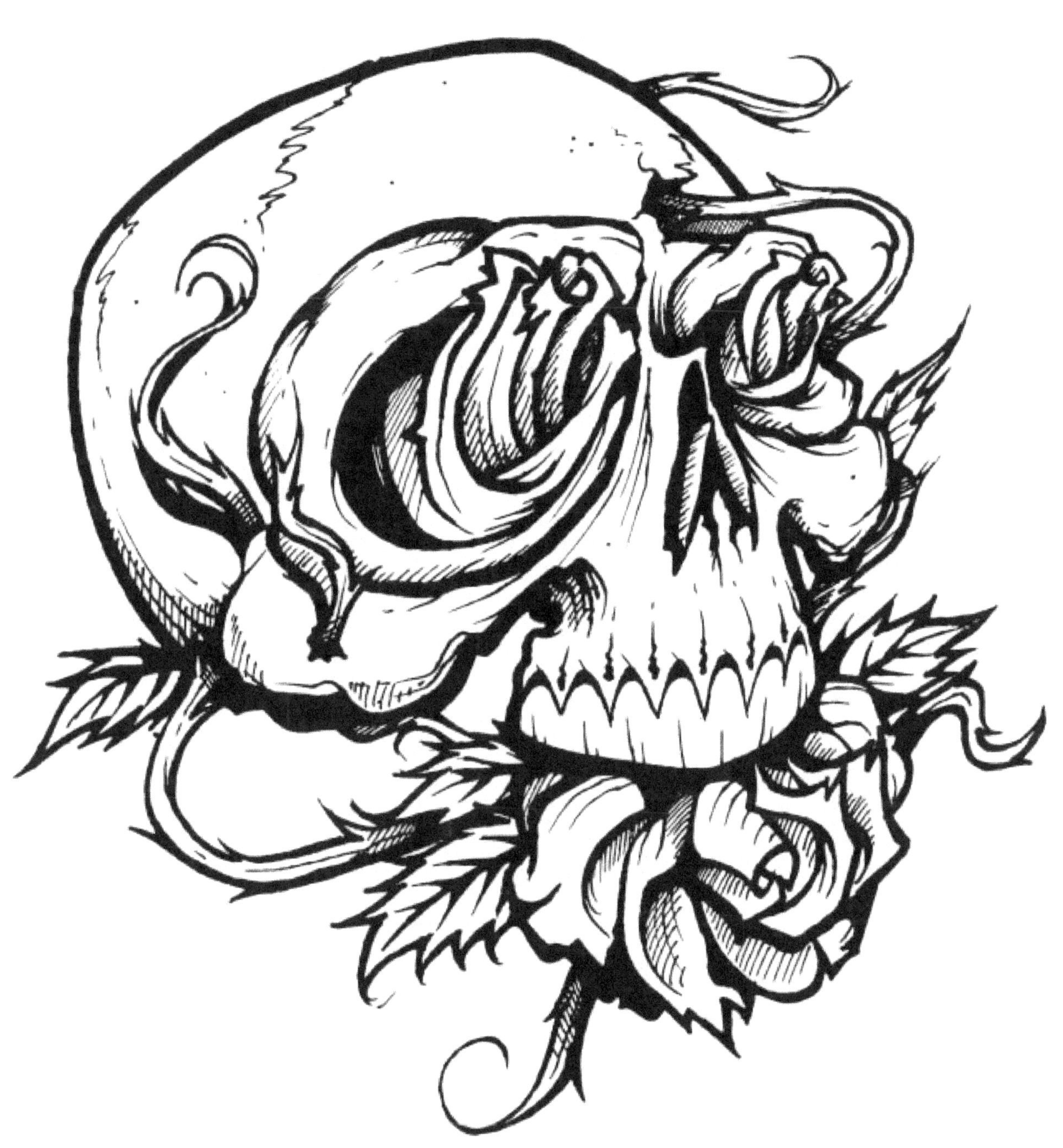

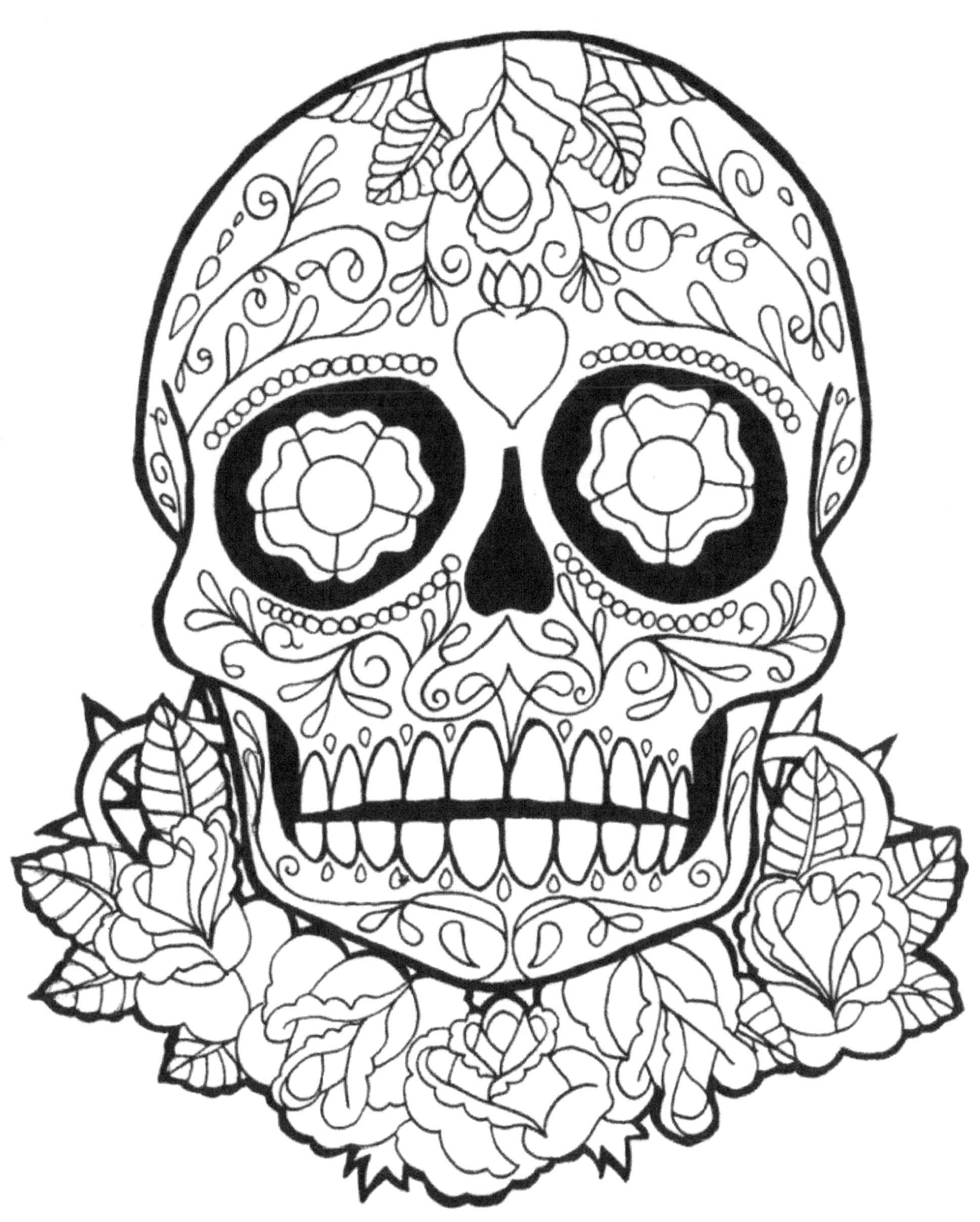

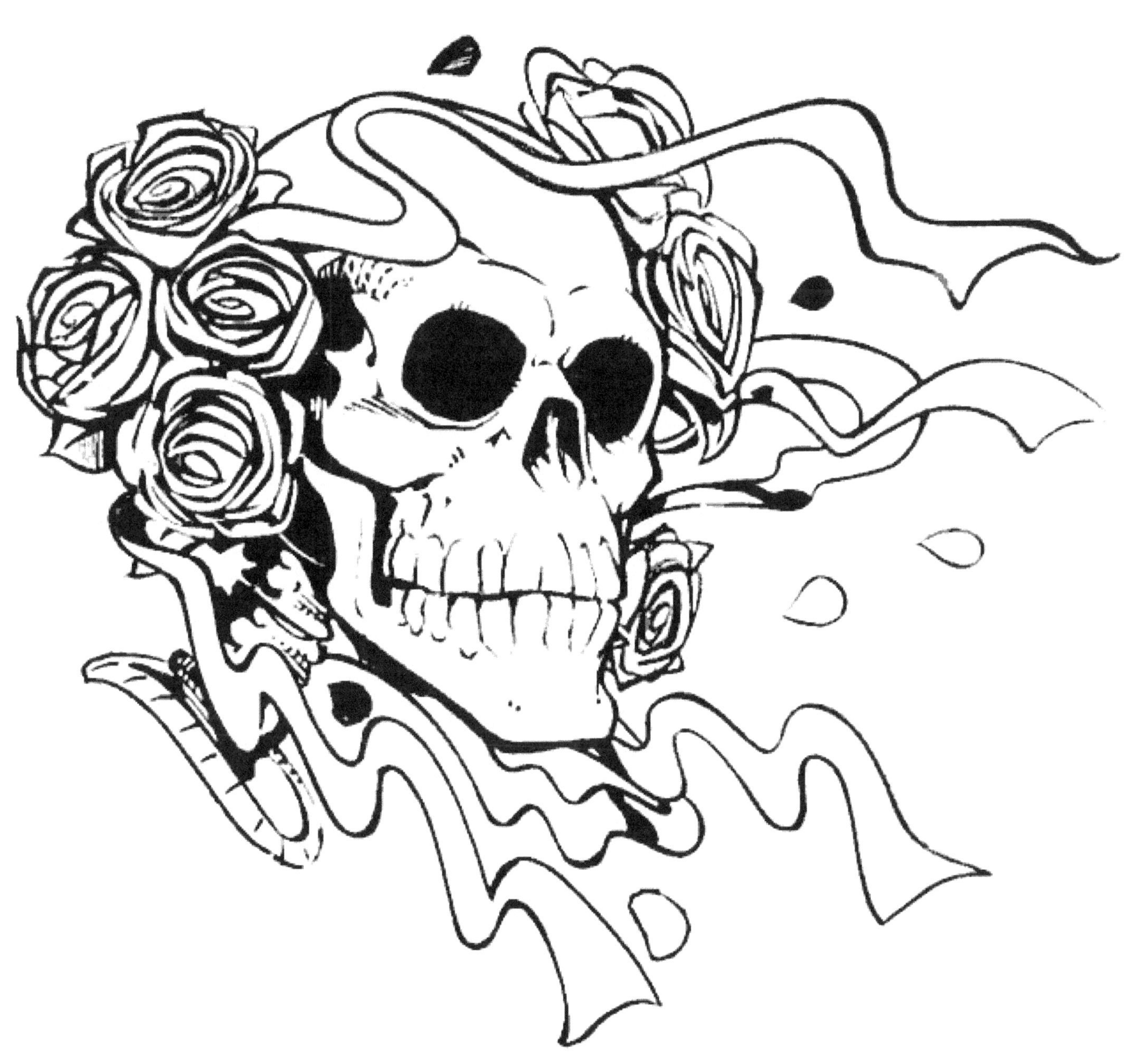

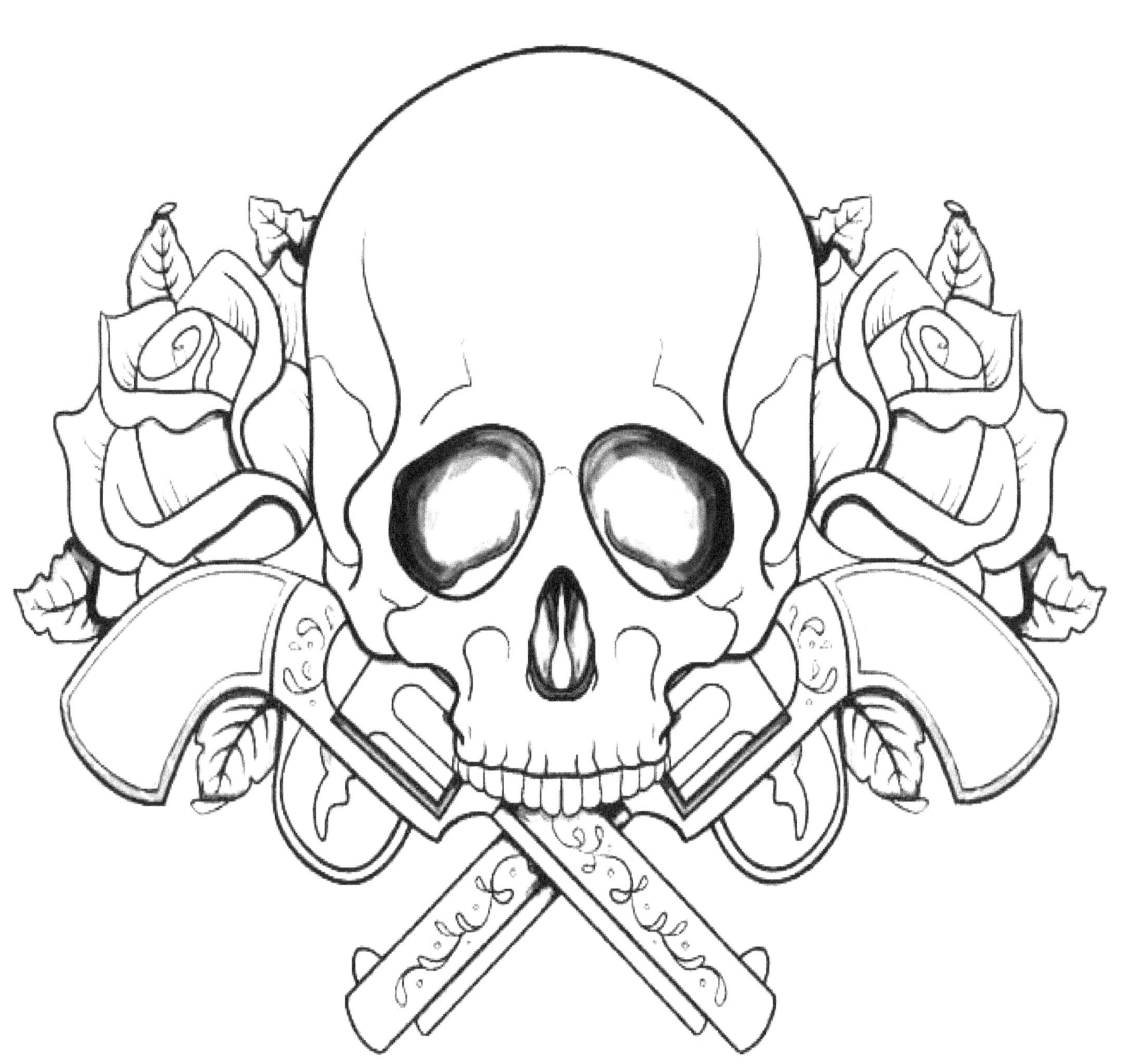

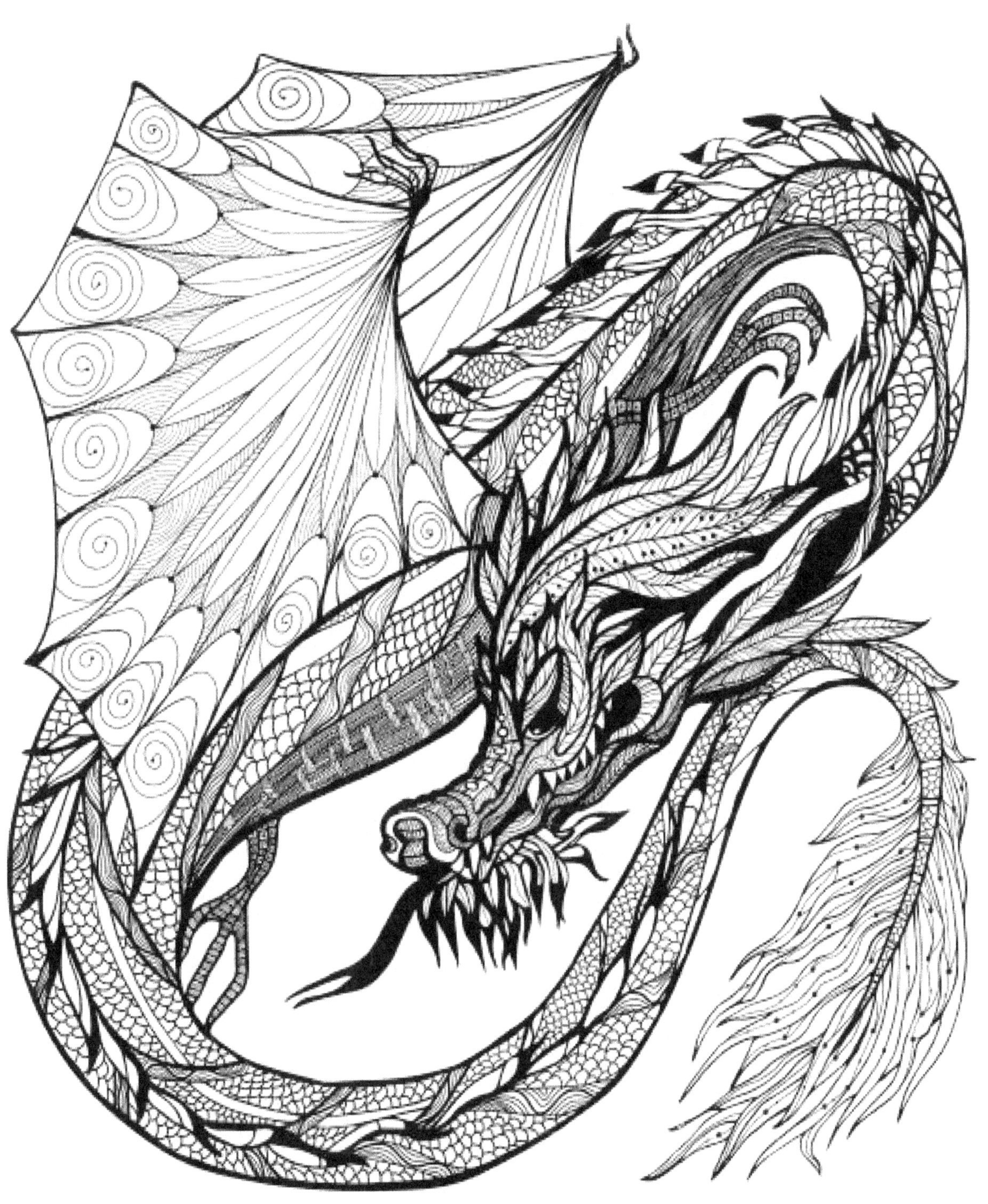

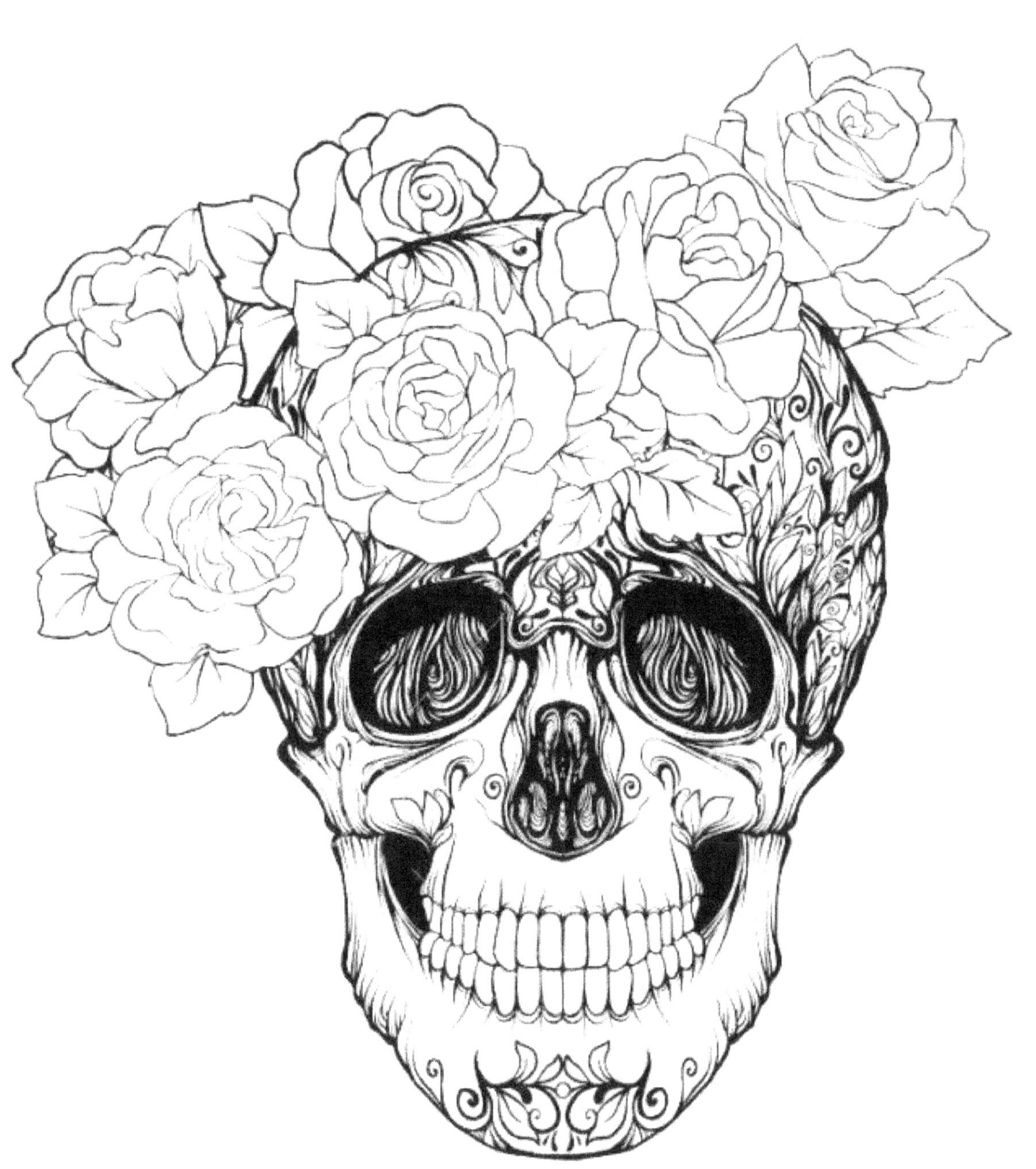

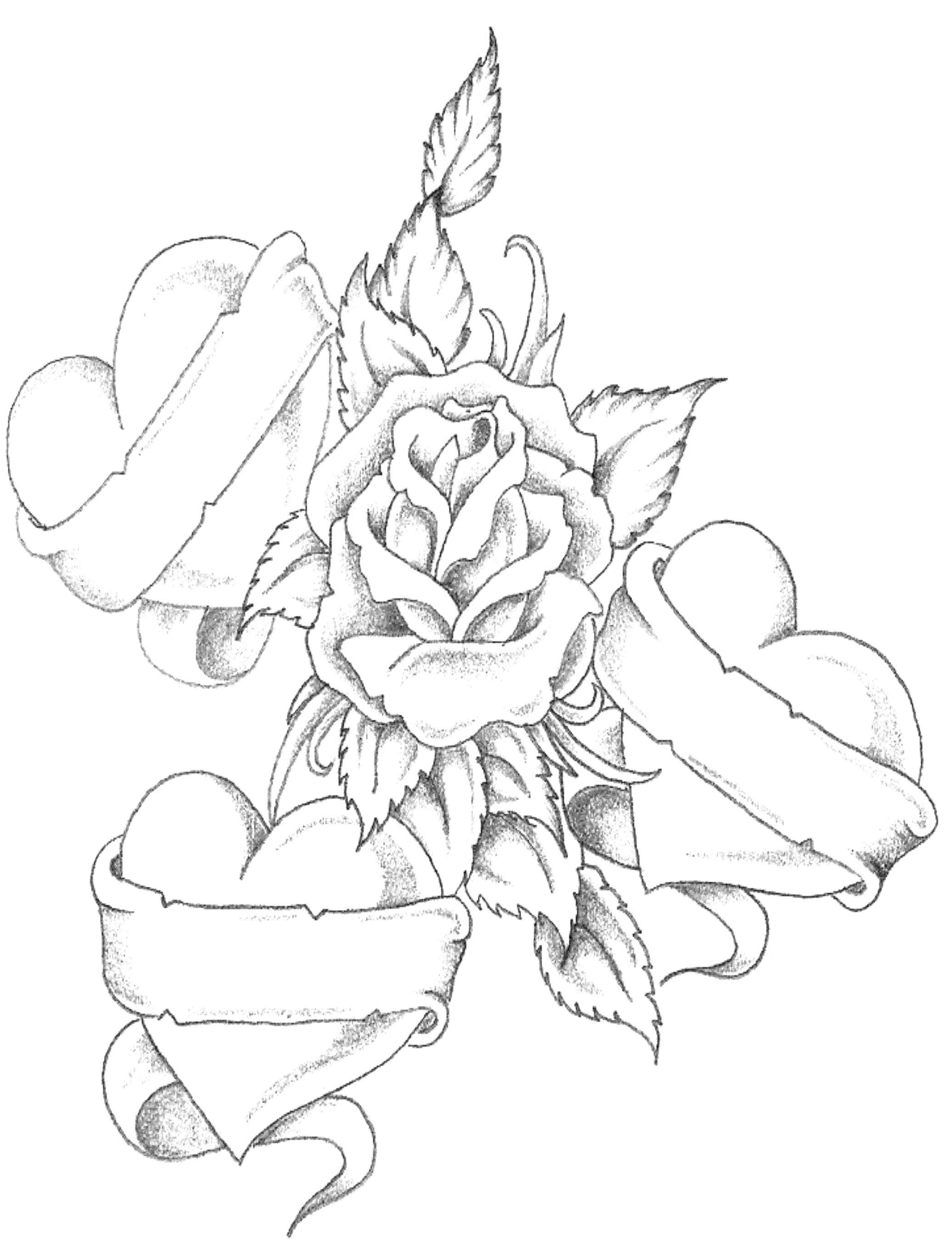

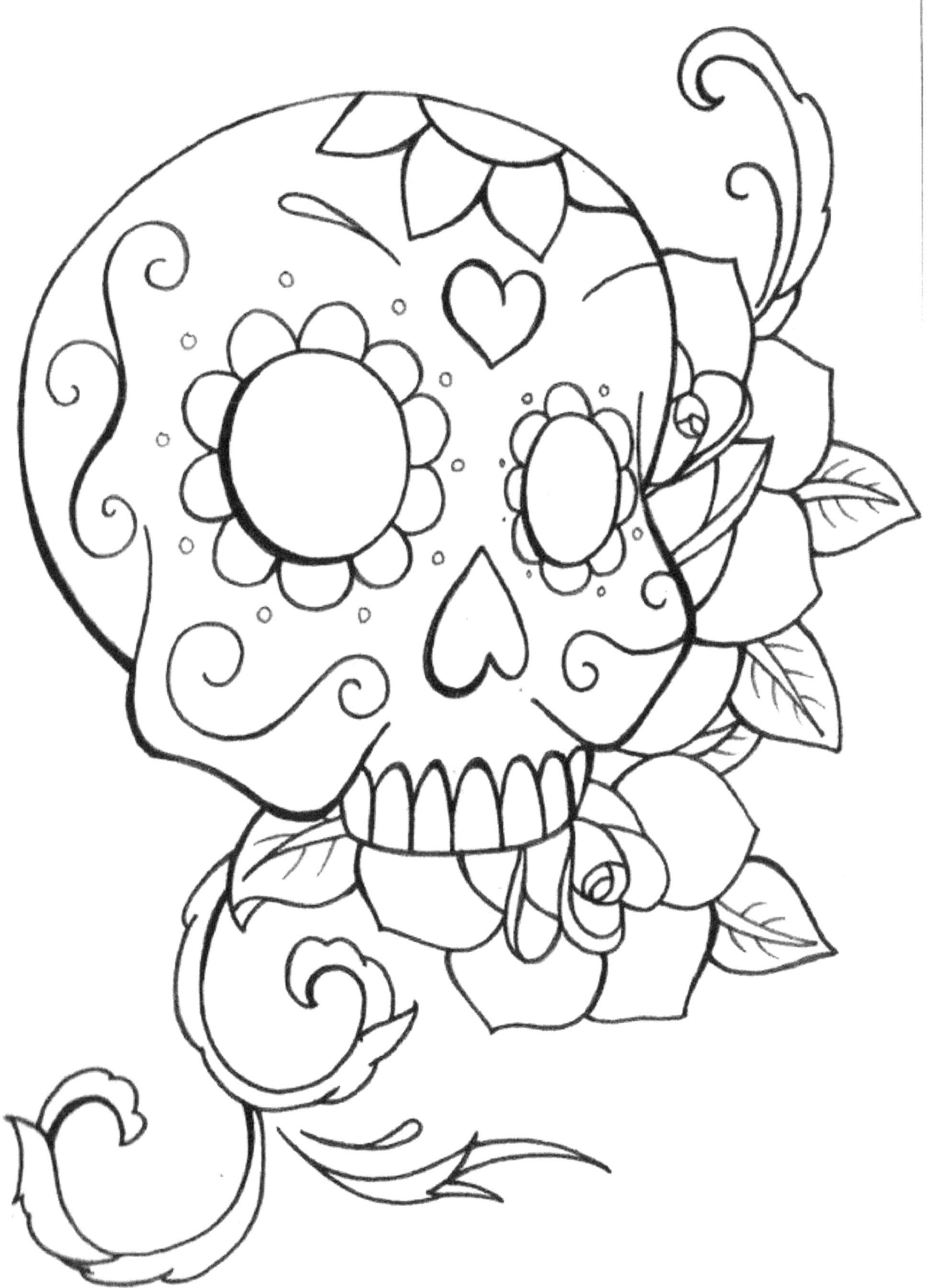

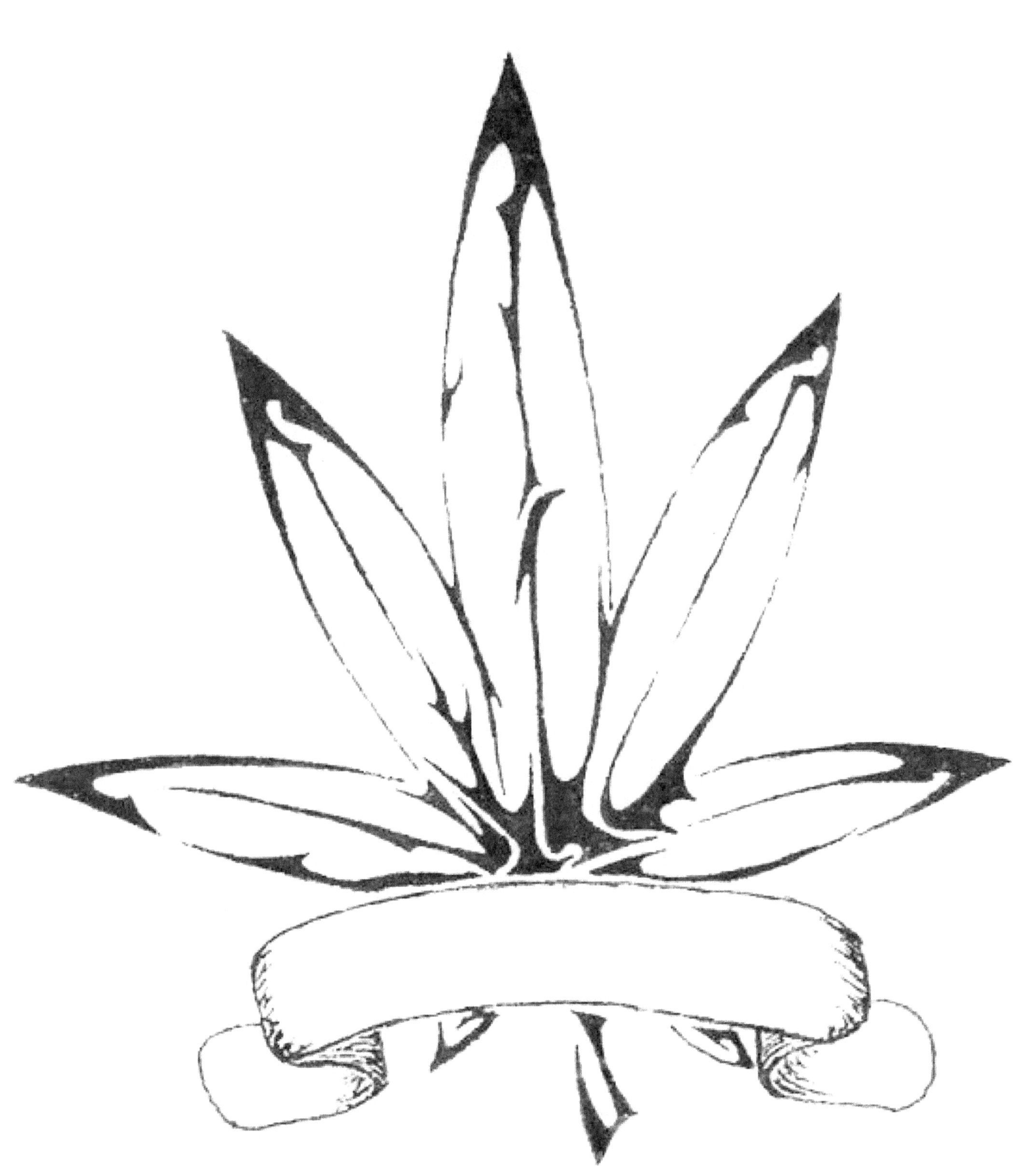

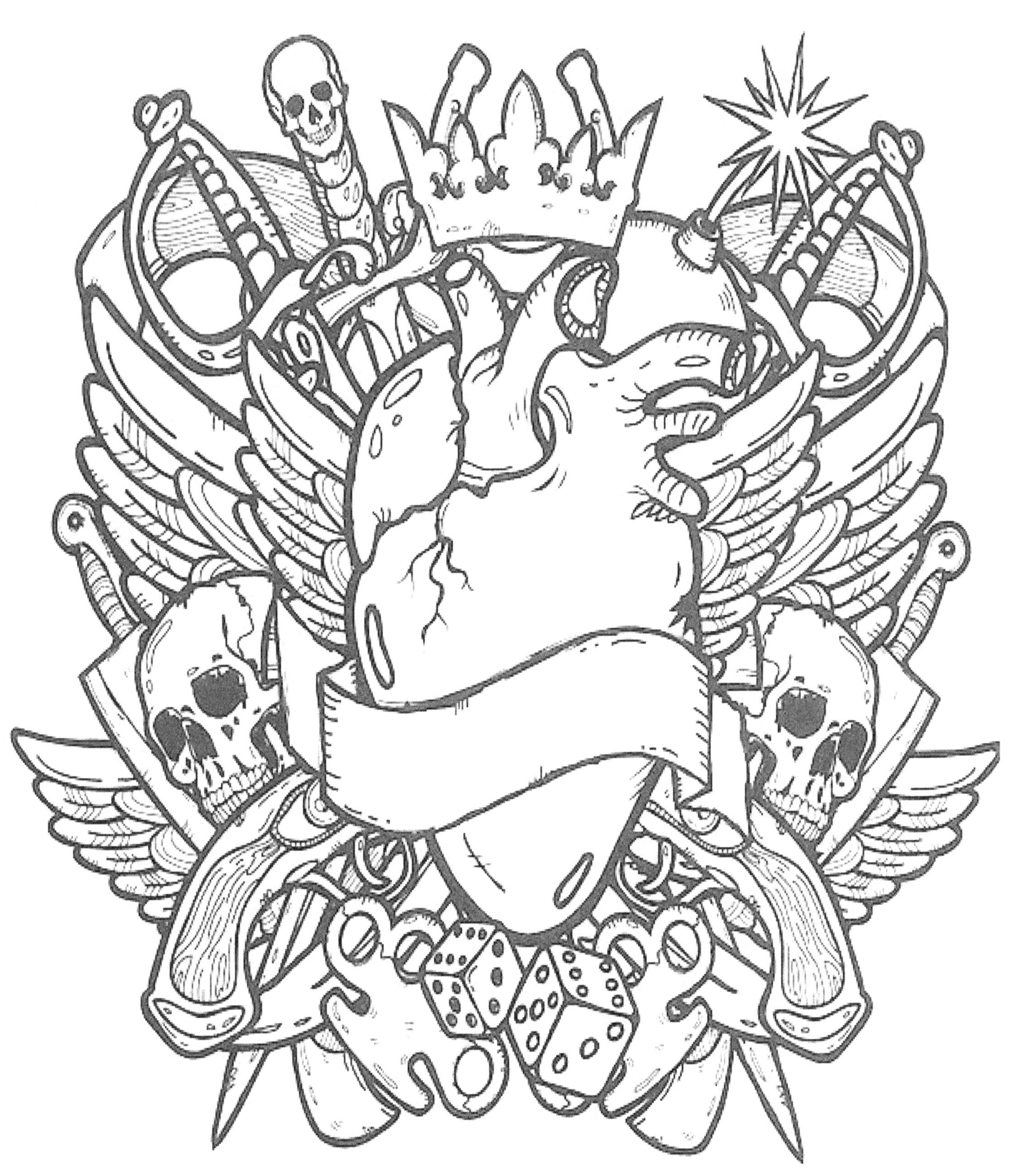

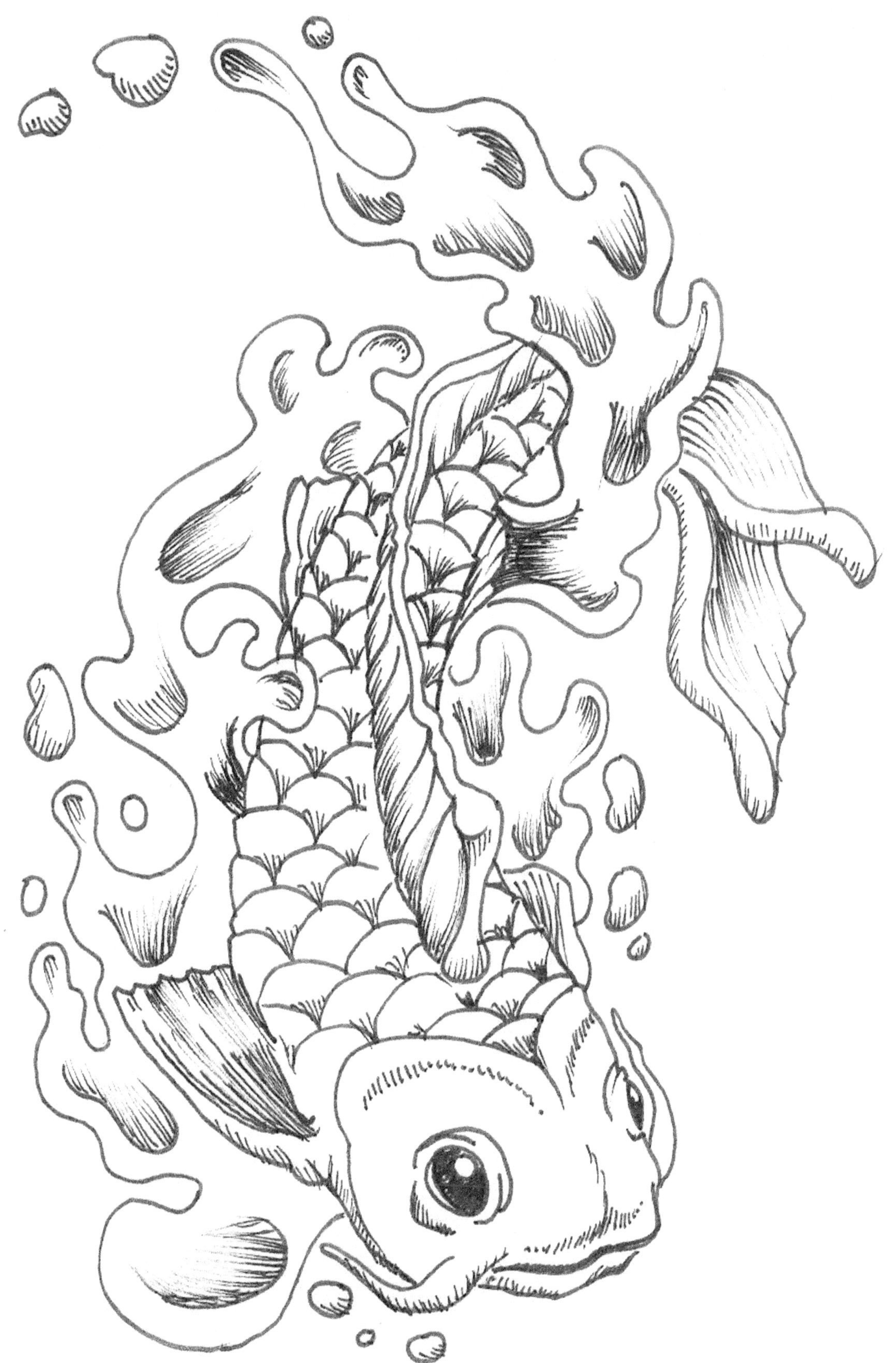

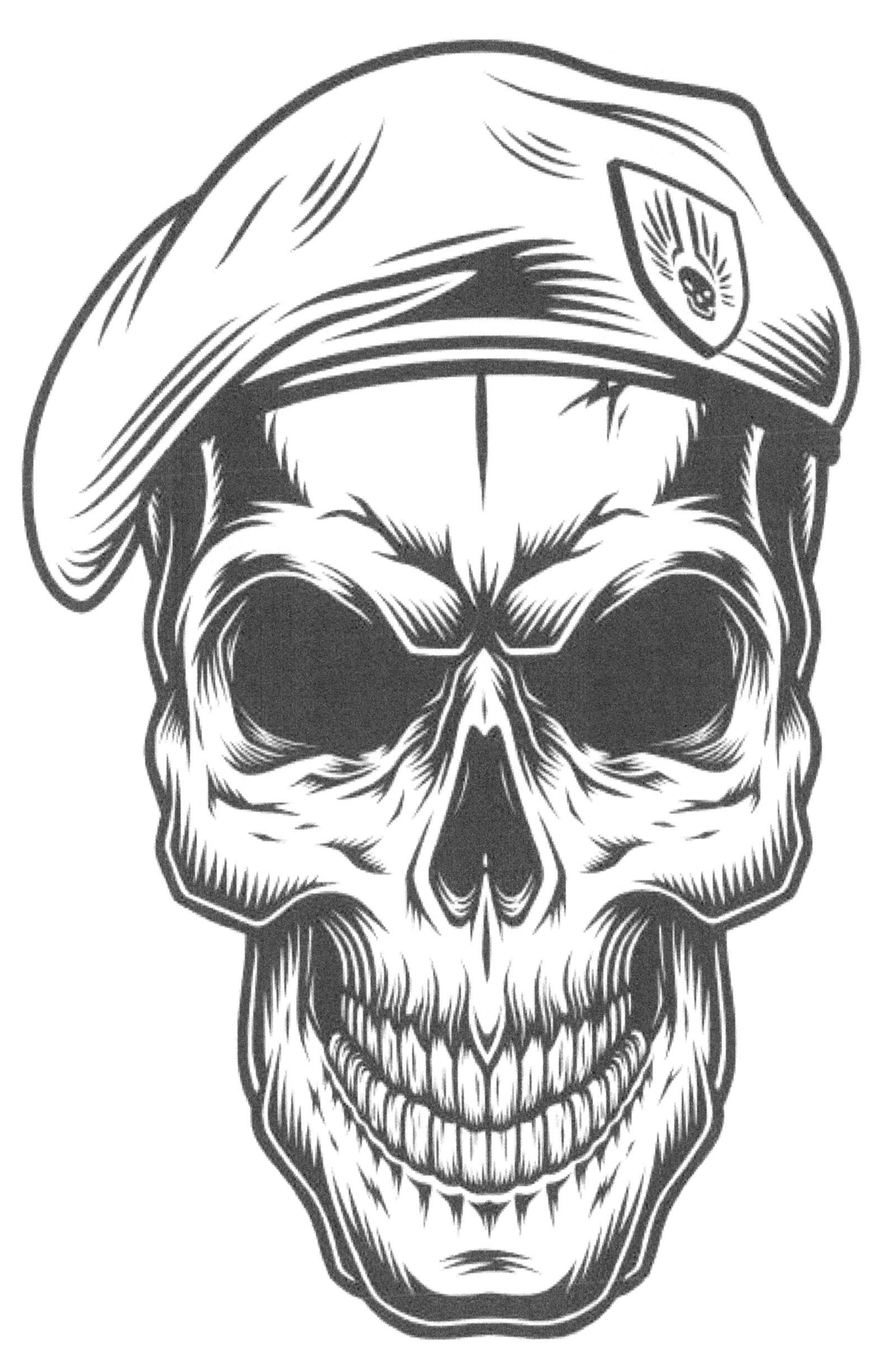

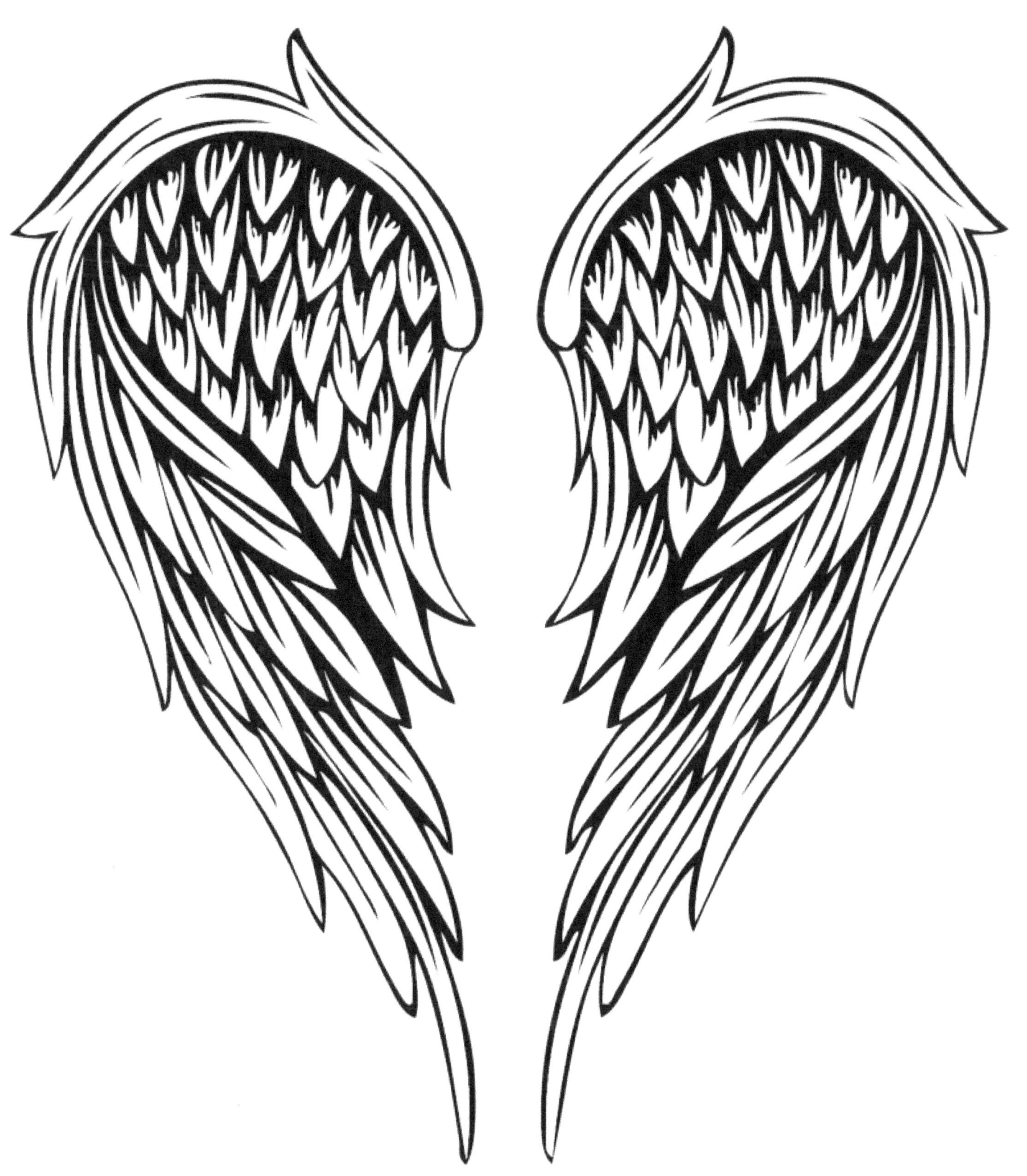

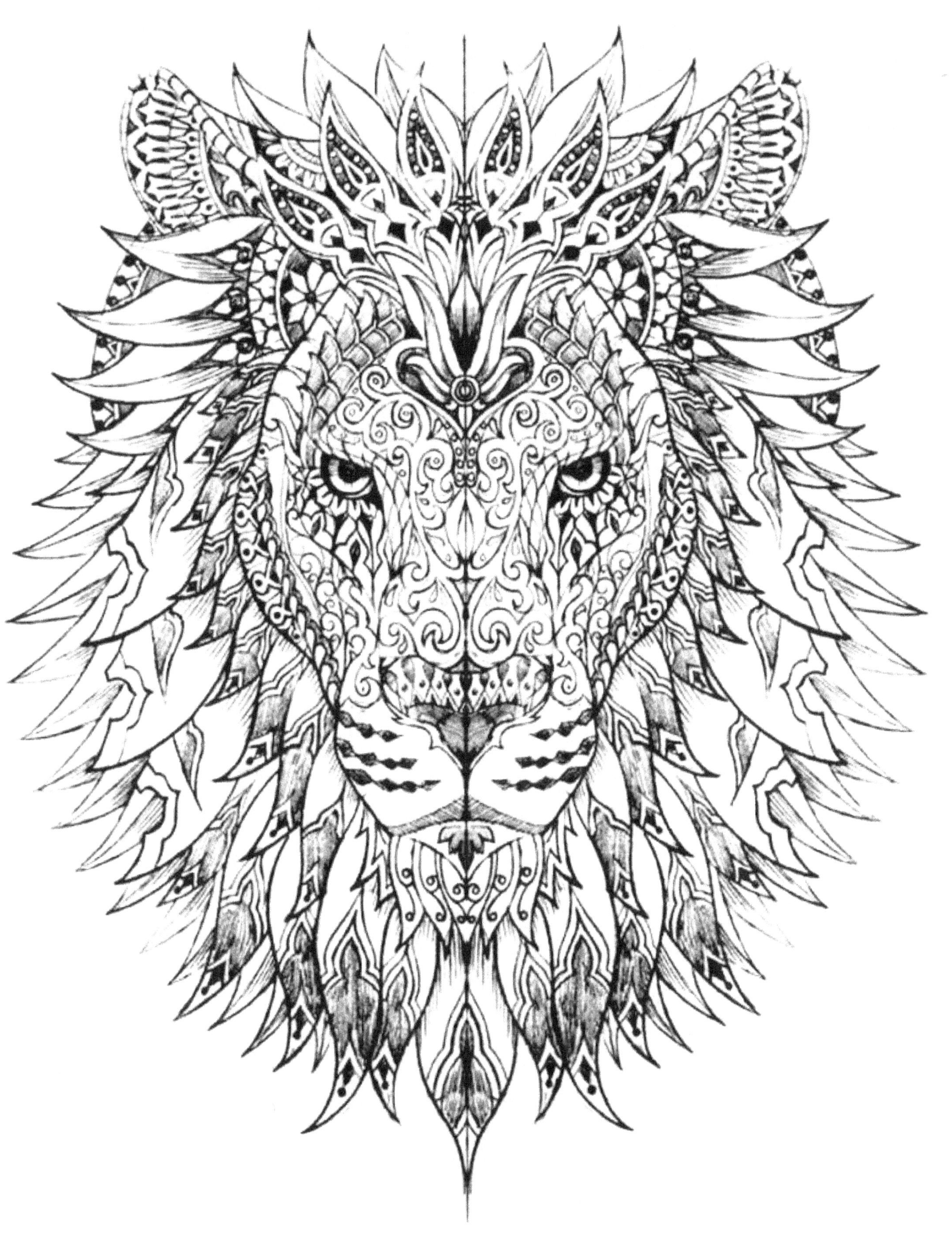

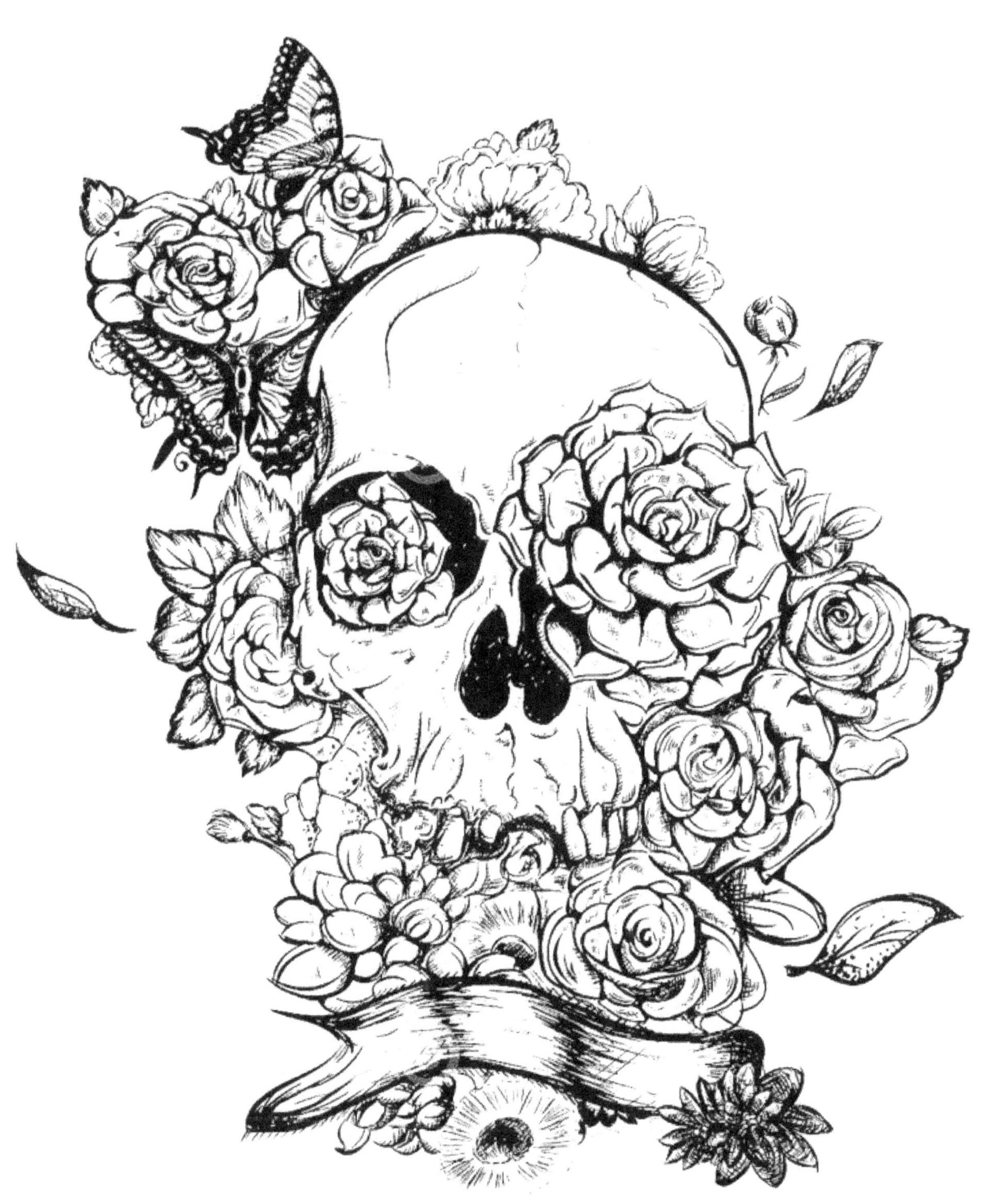

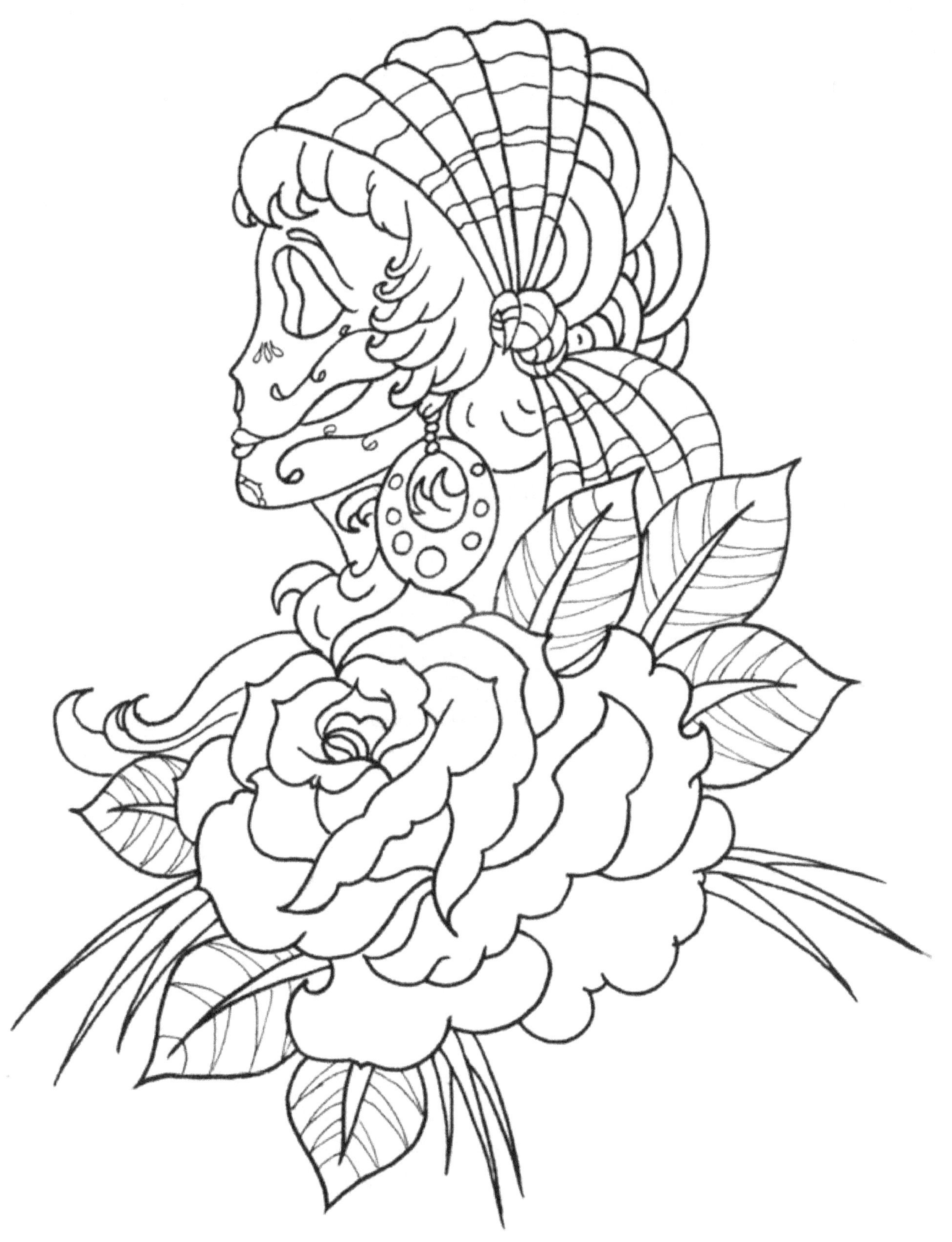

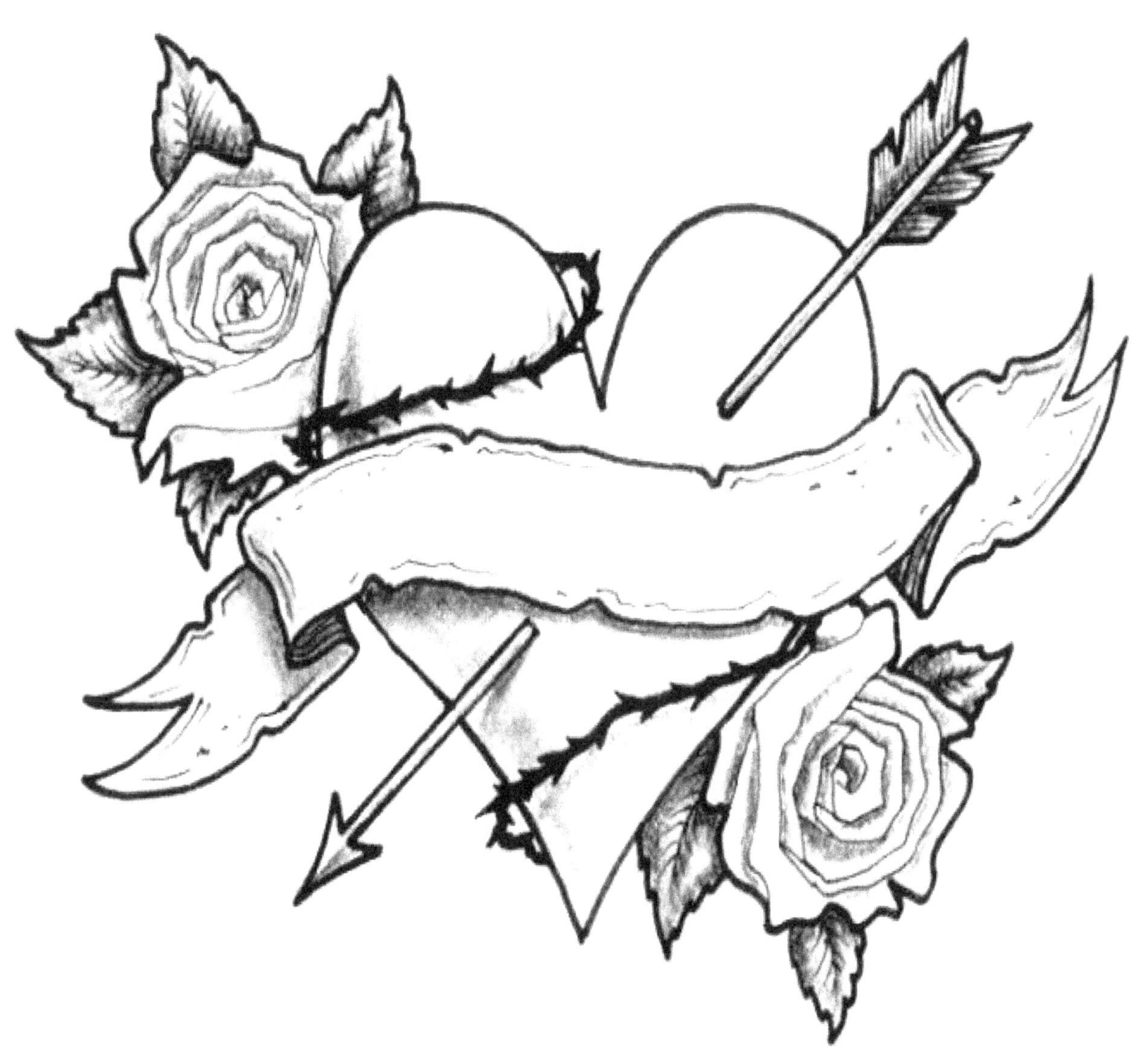

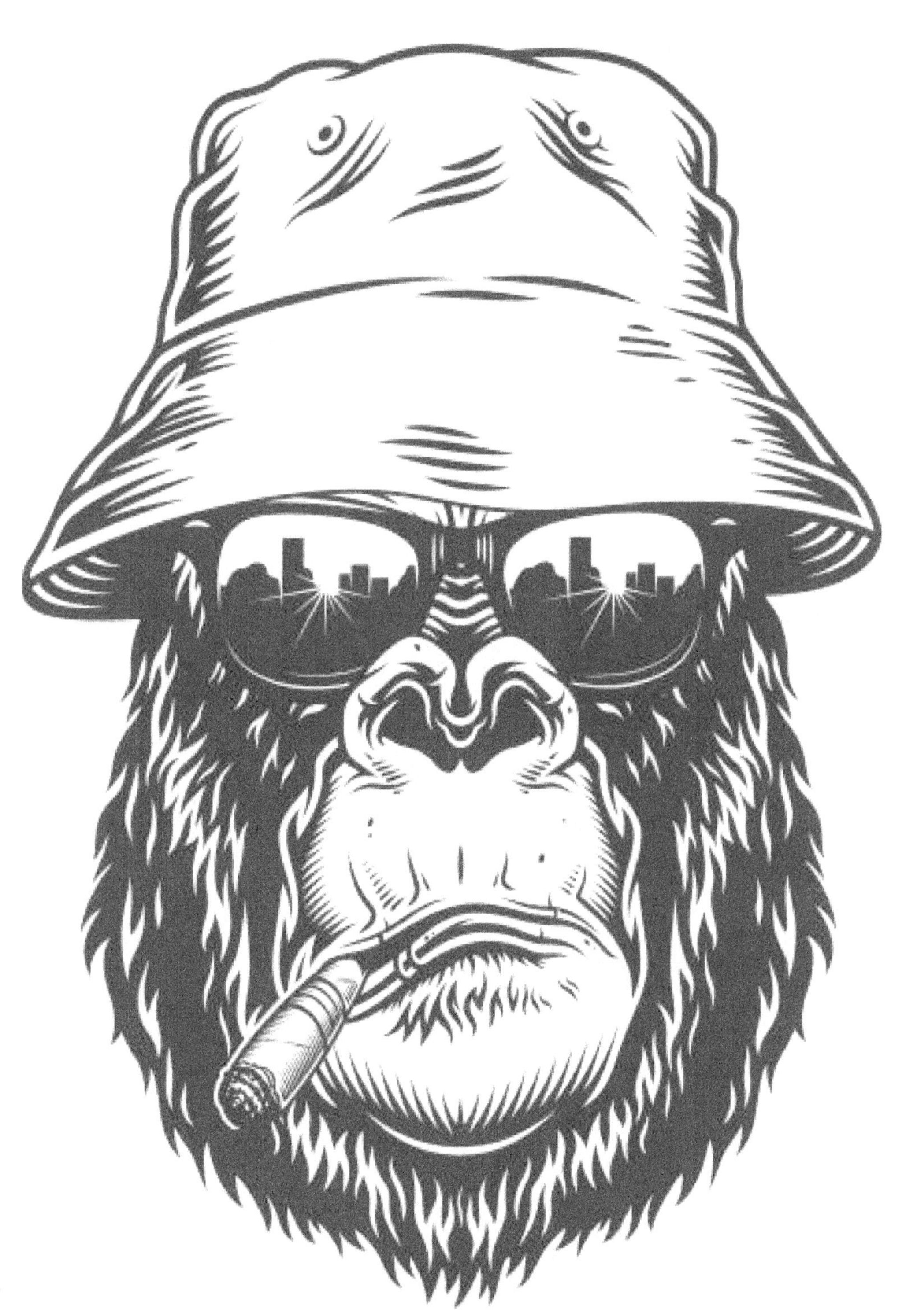

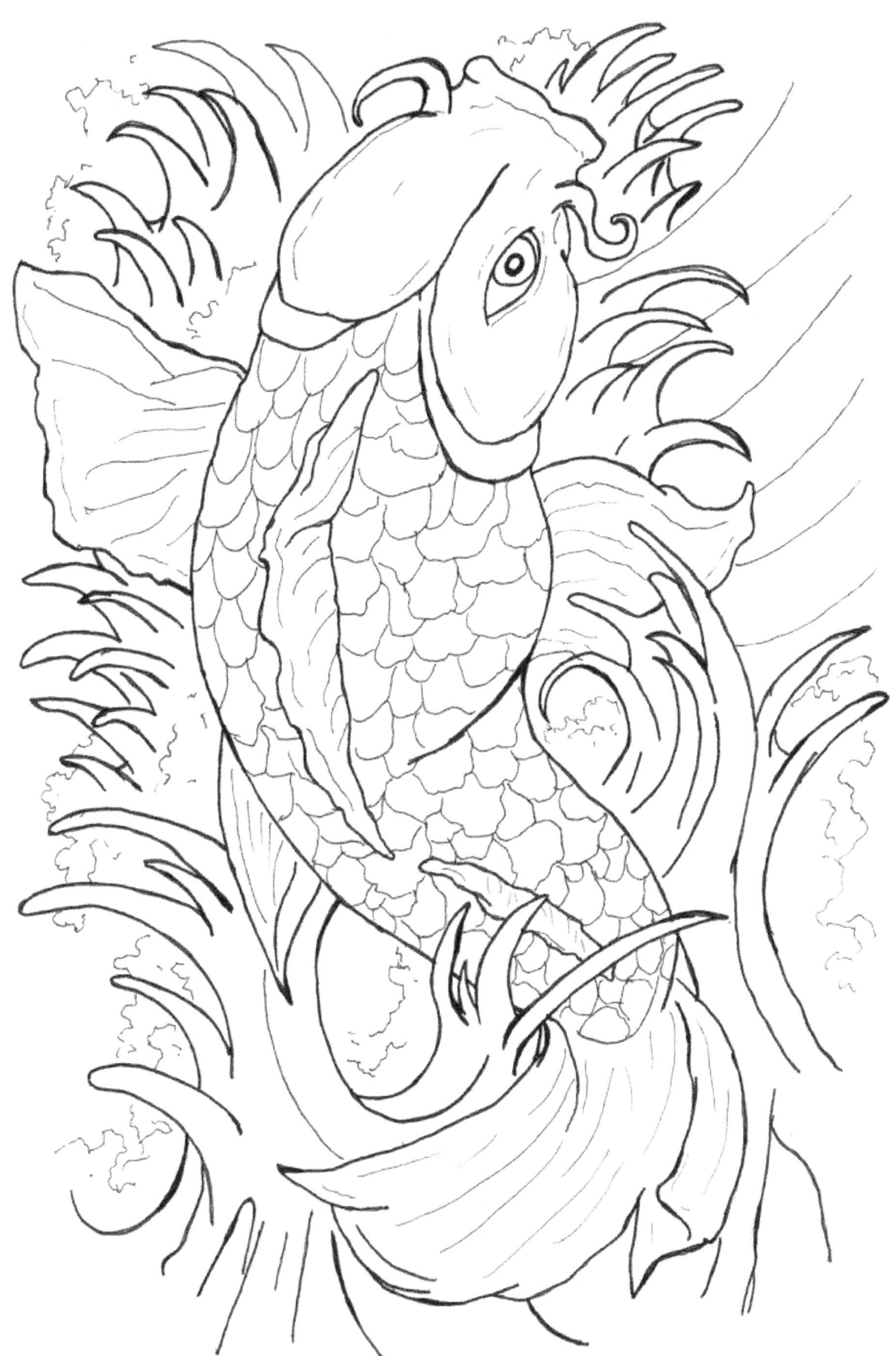

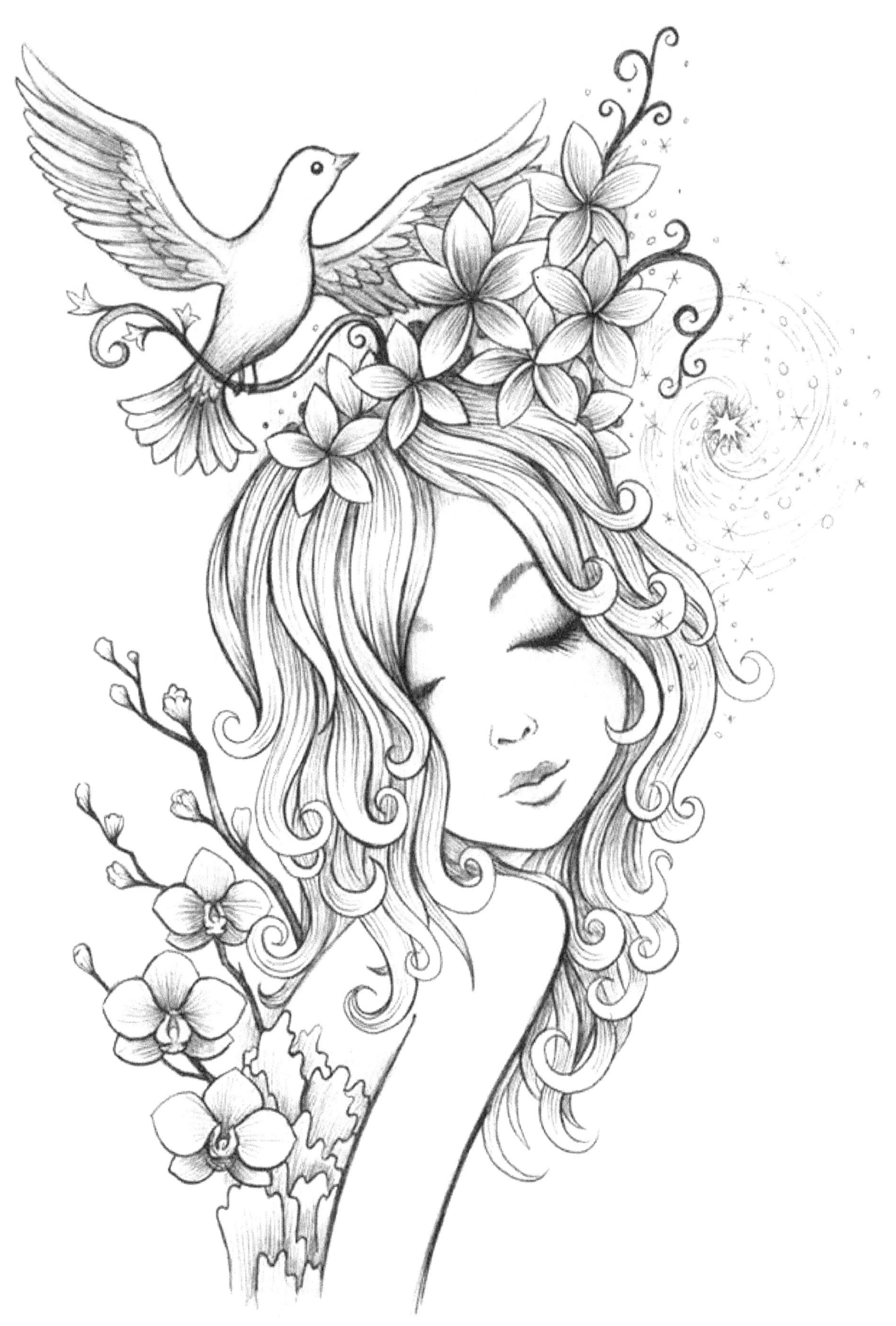

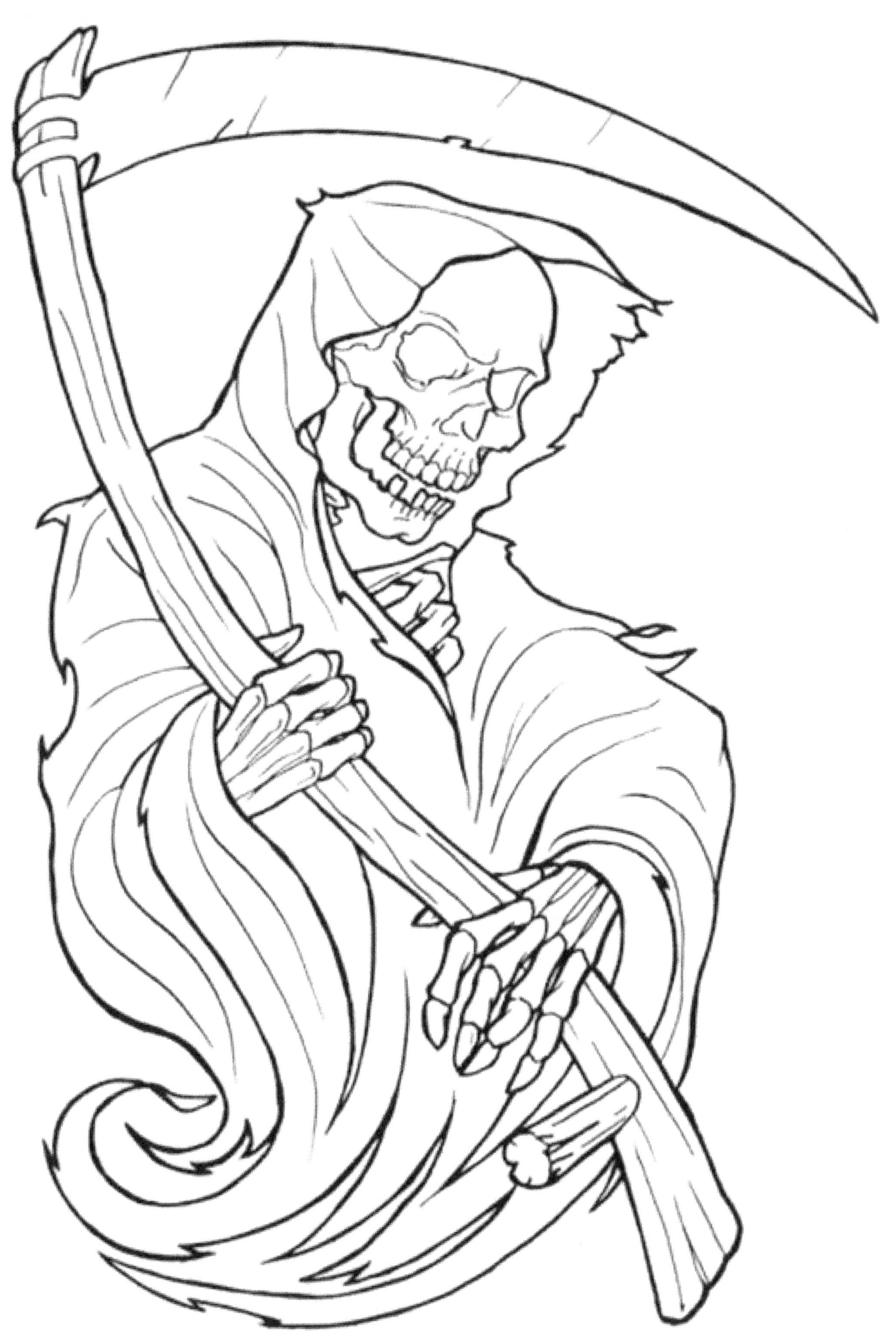

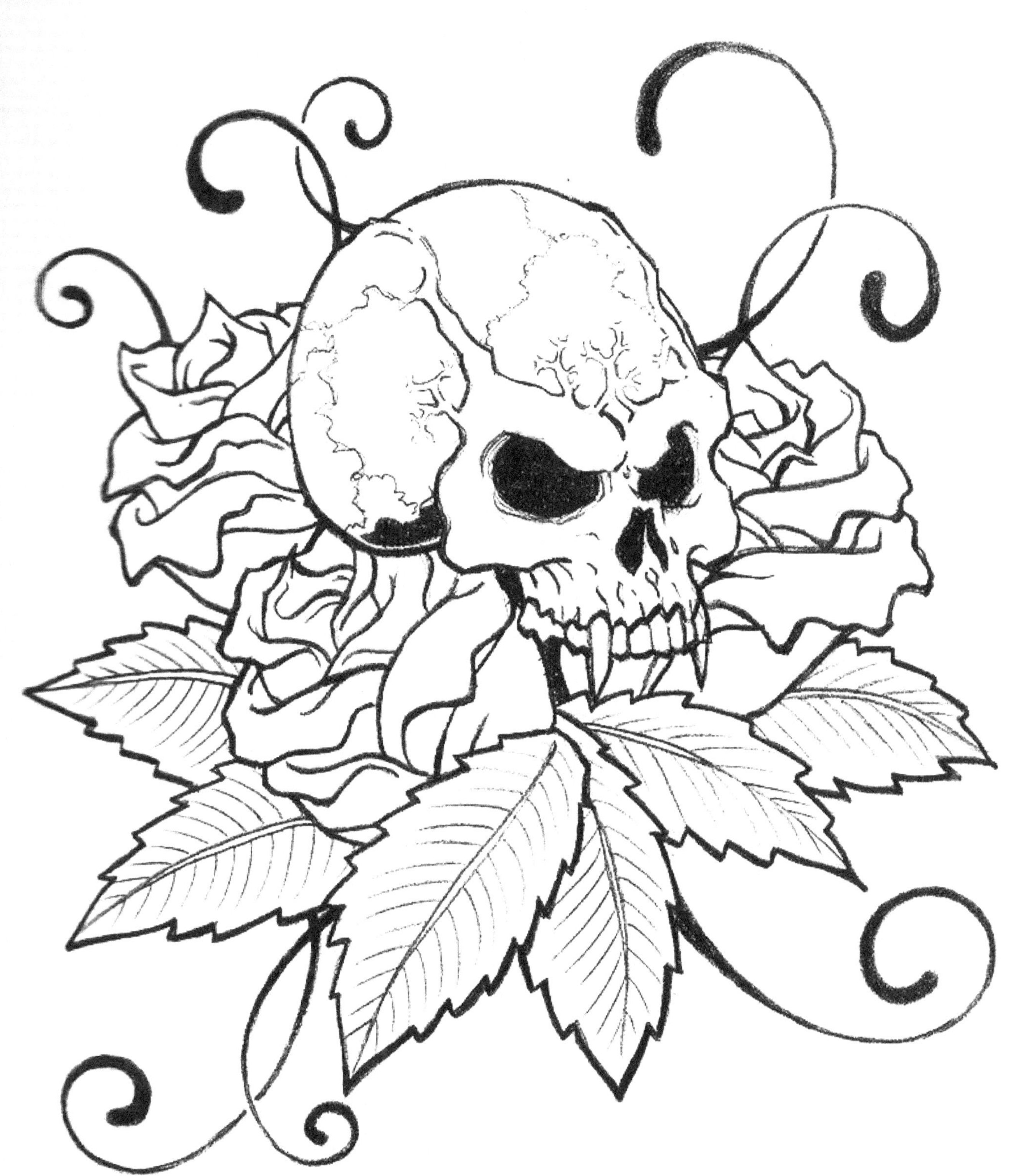

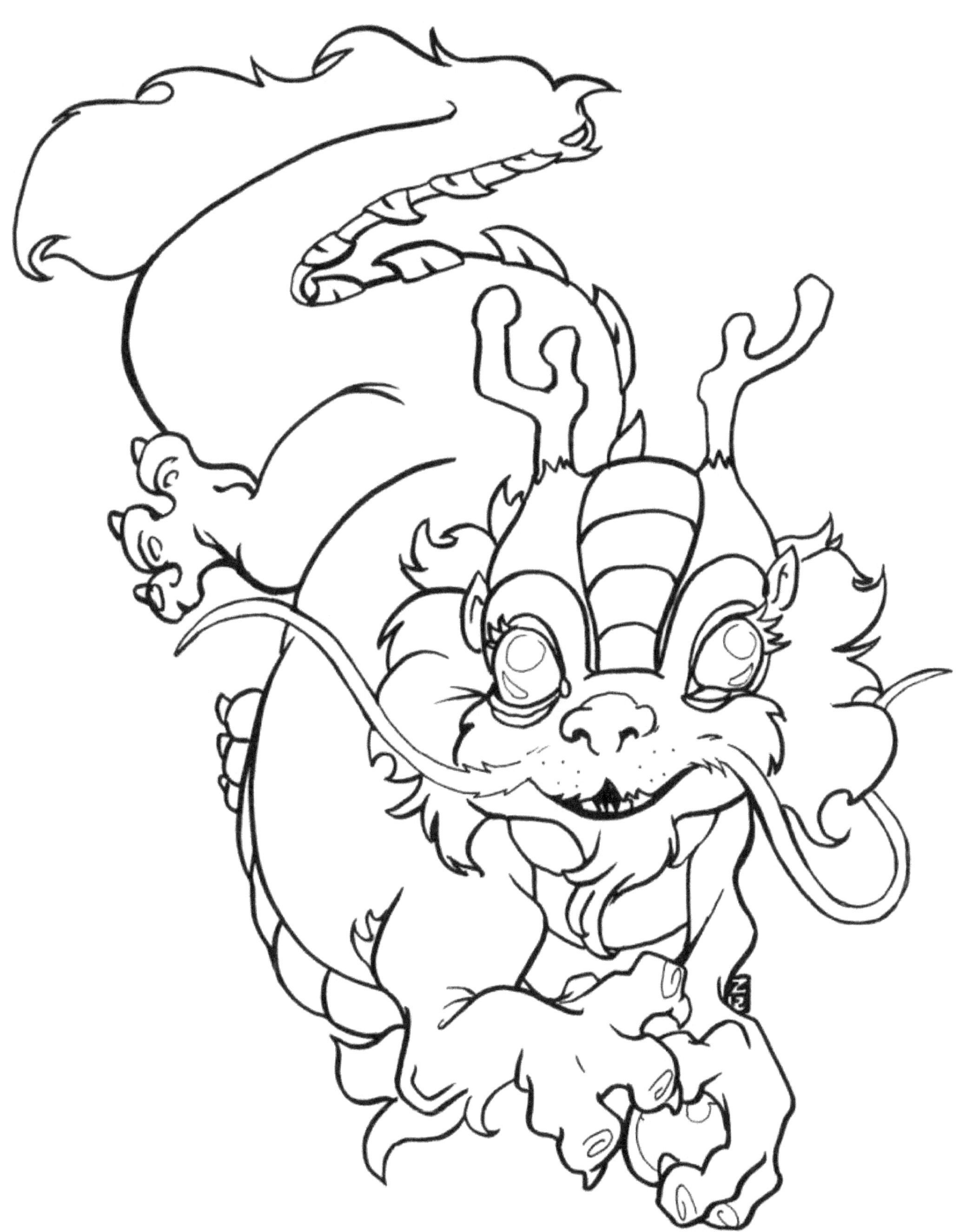

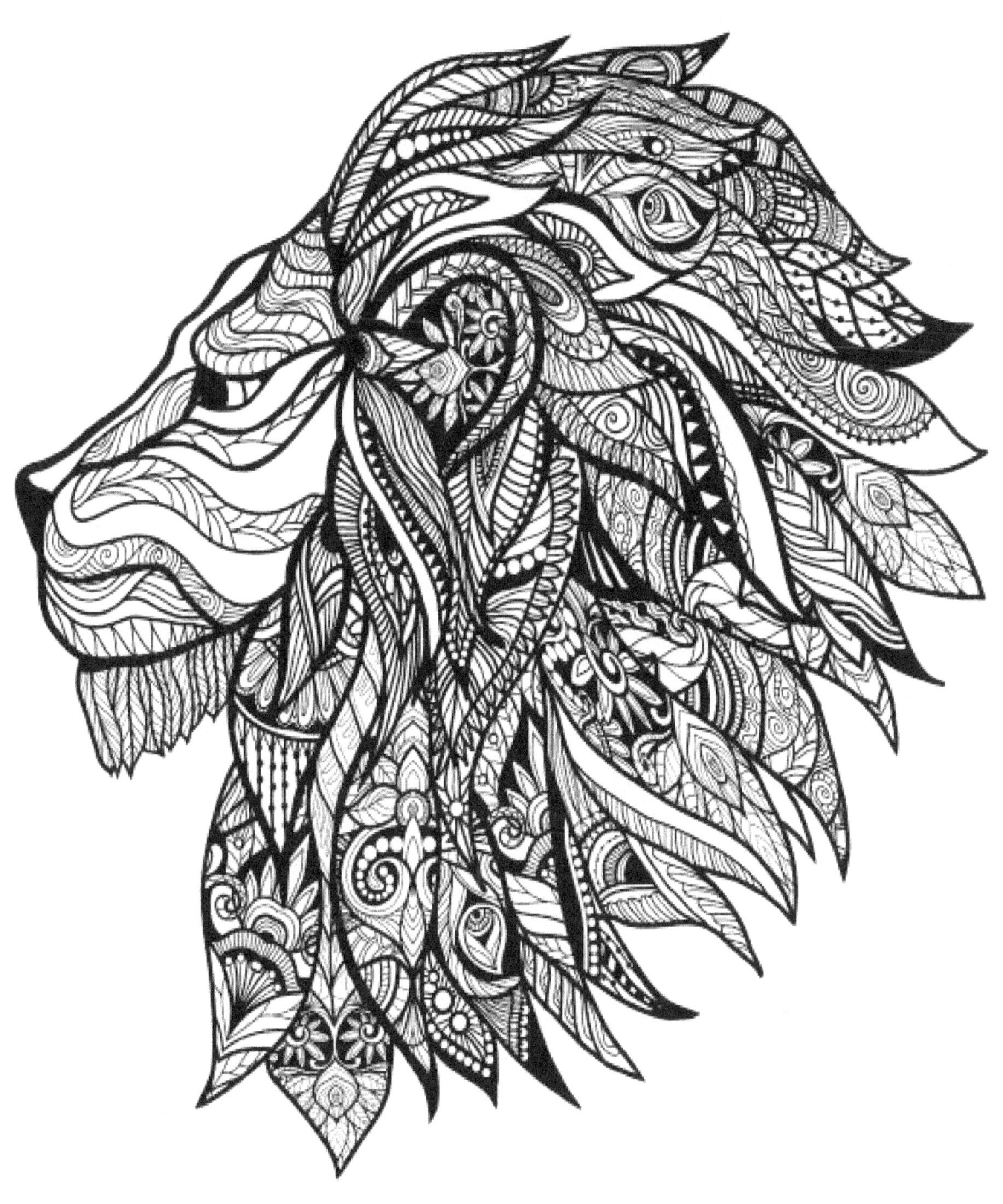

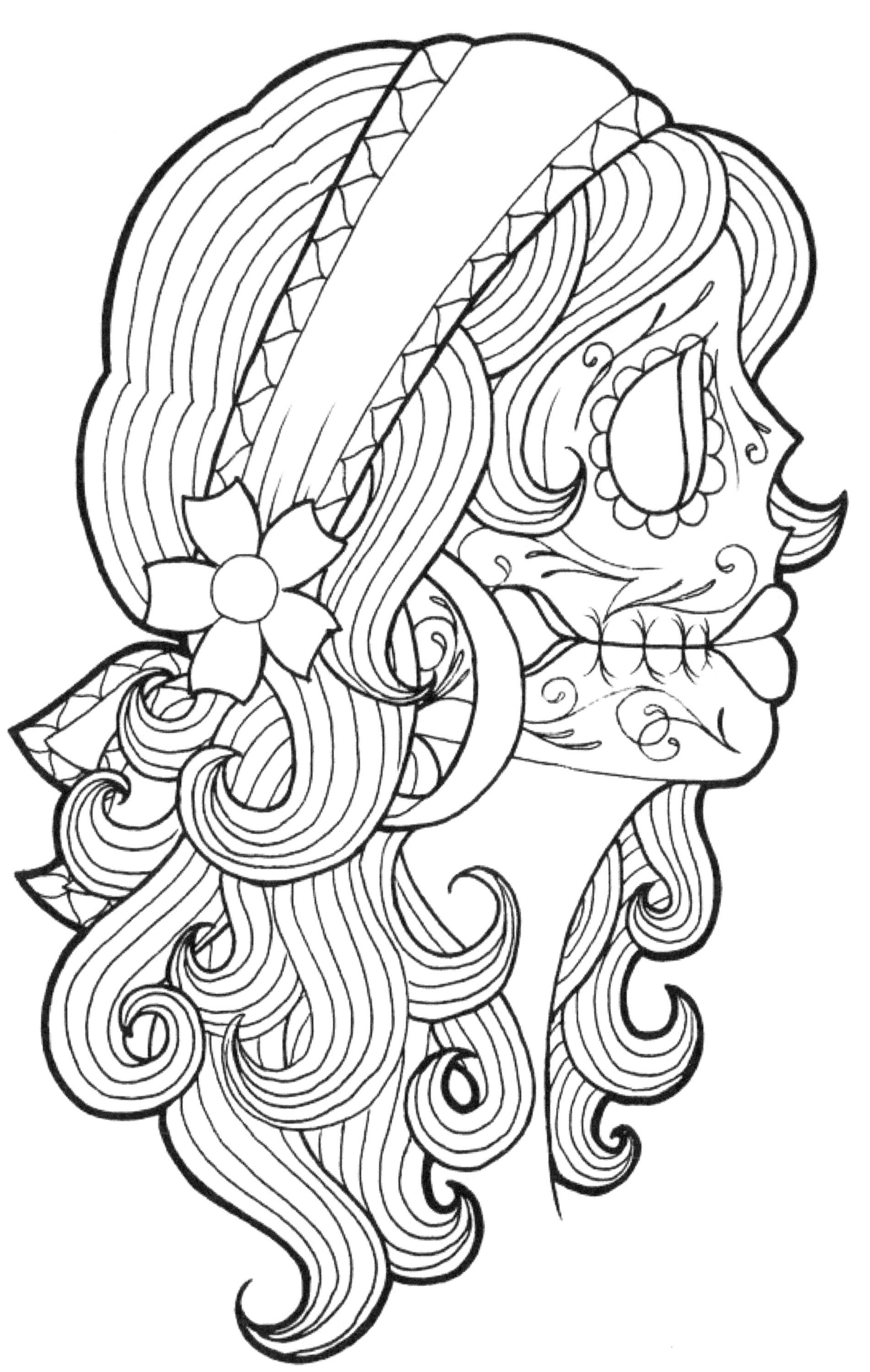

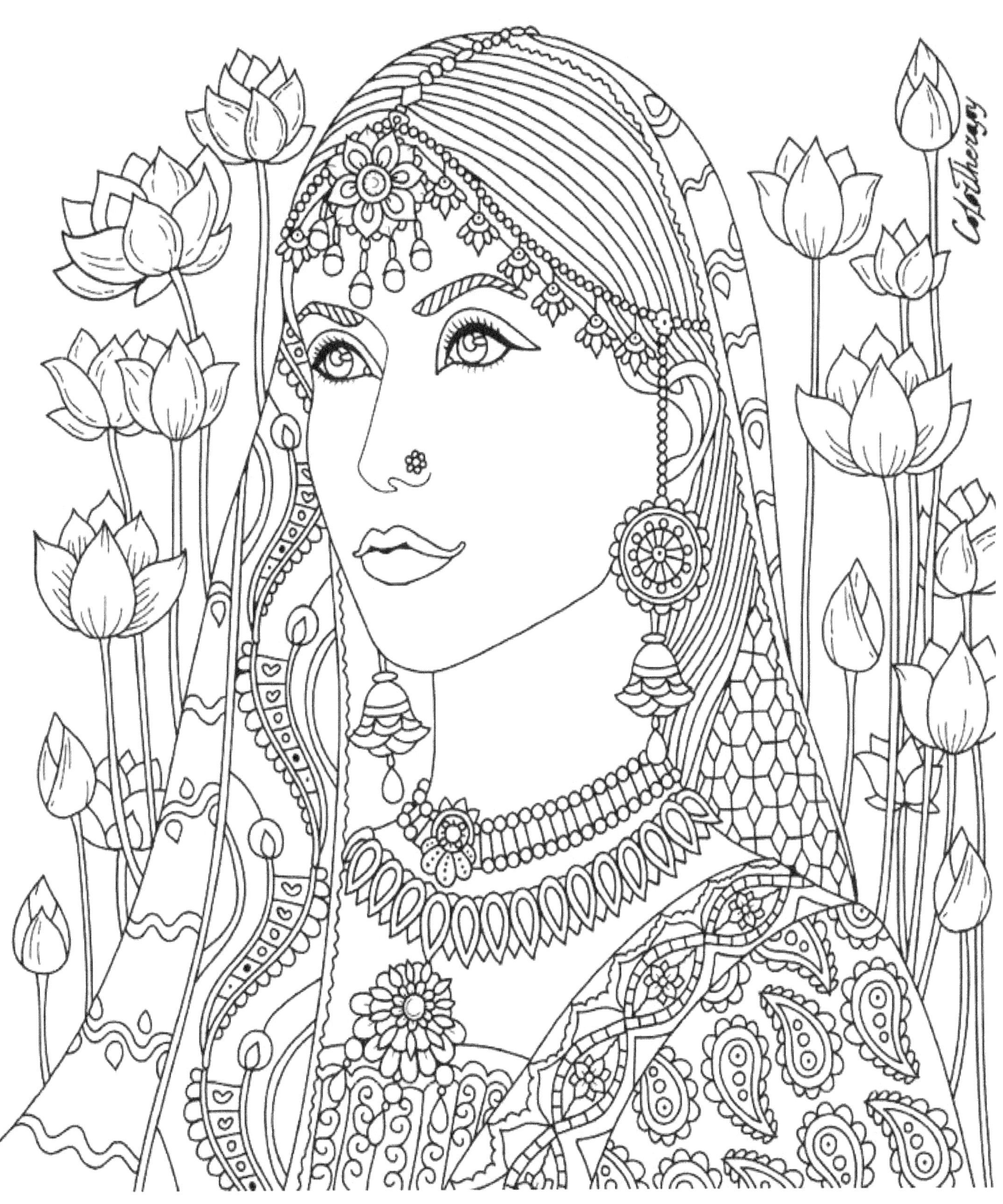
Coptherapy

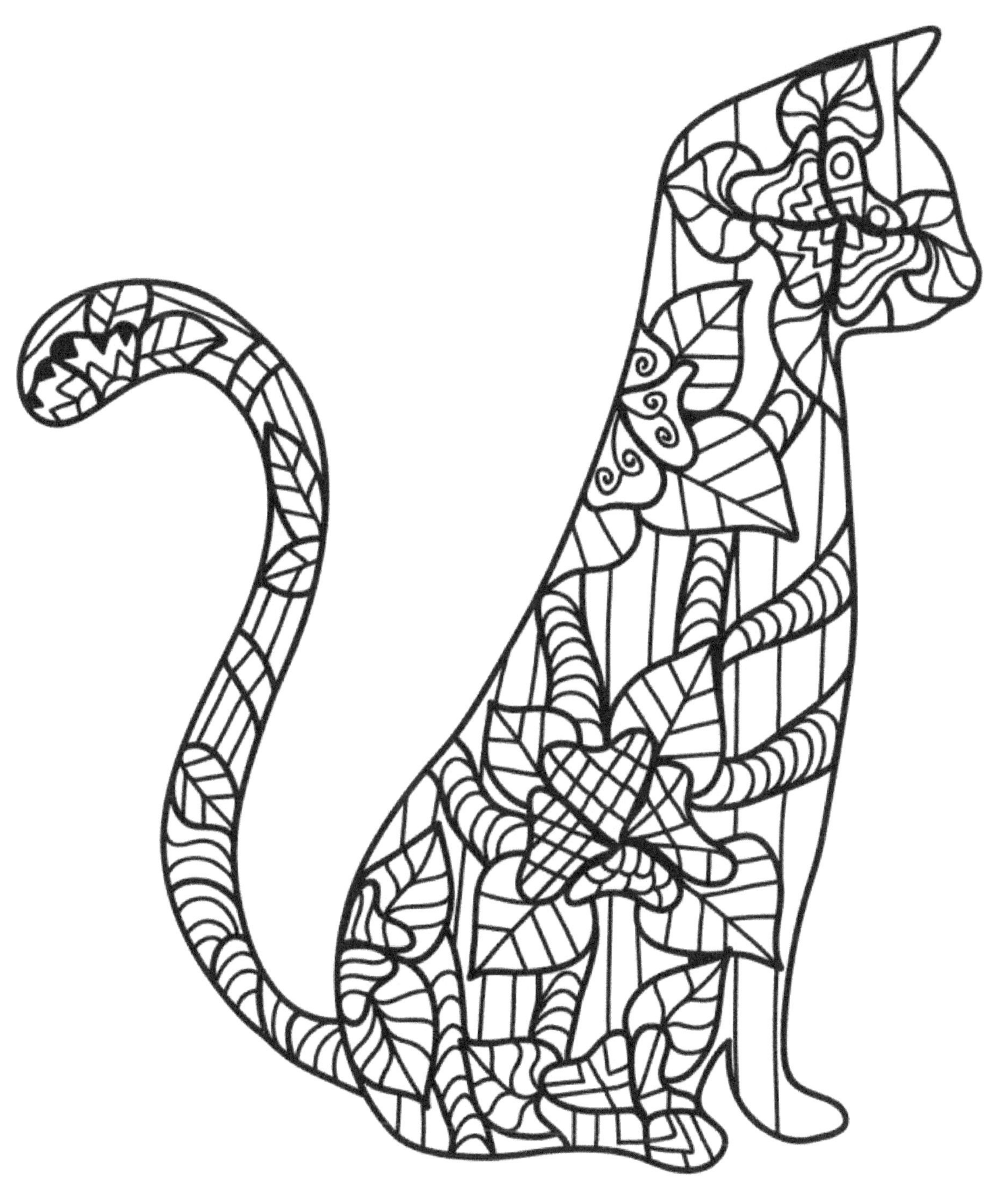

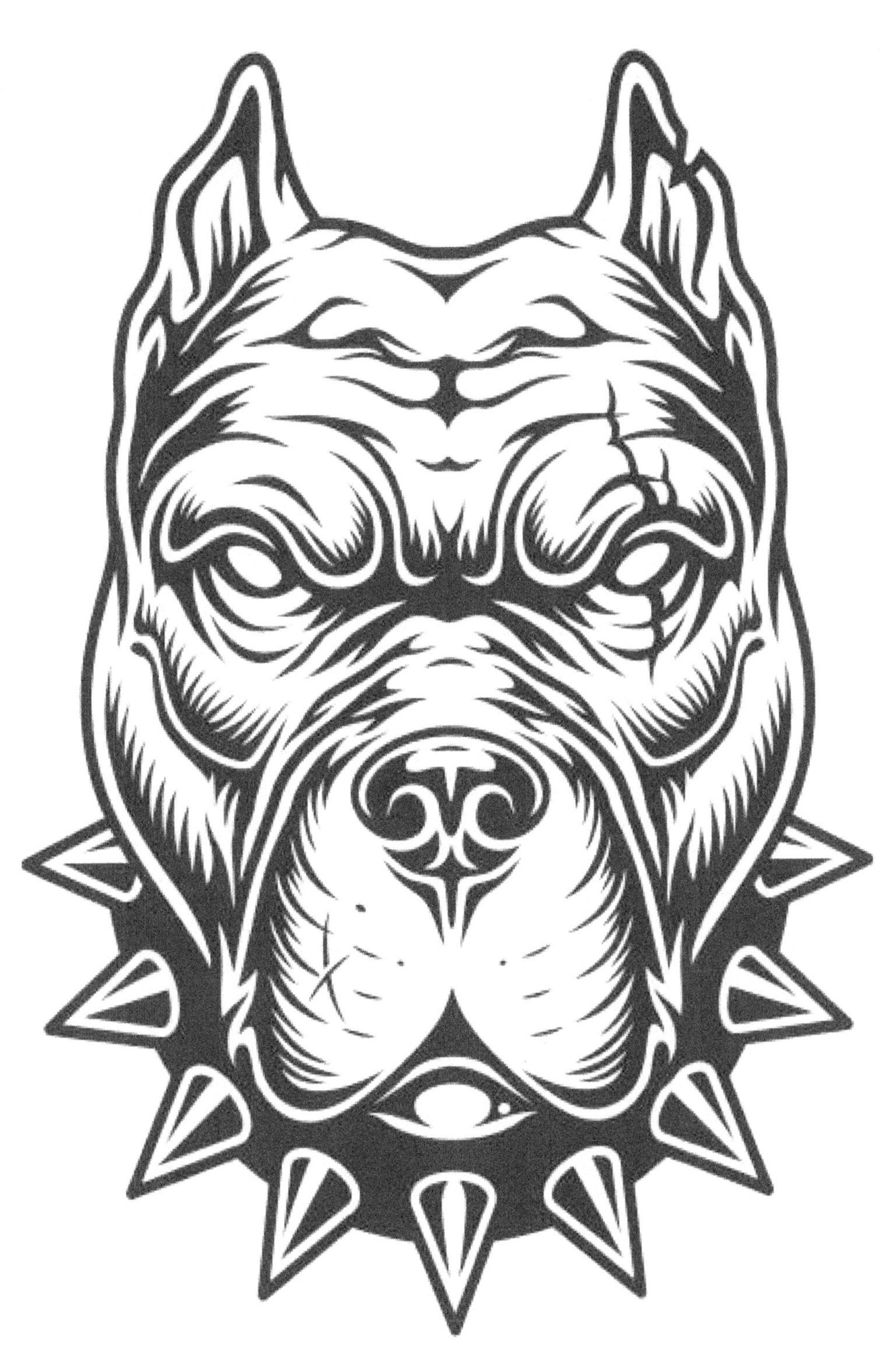

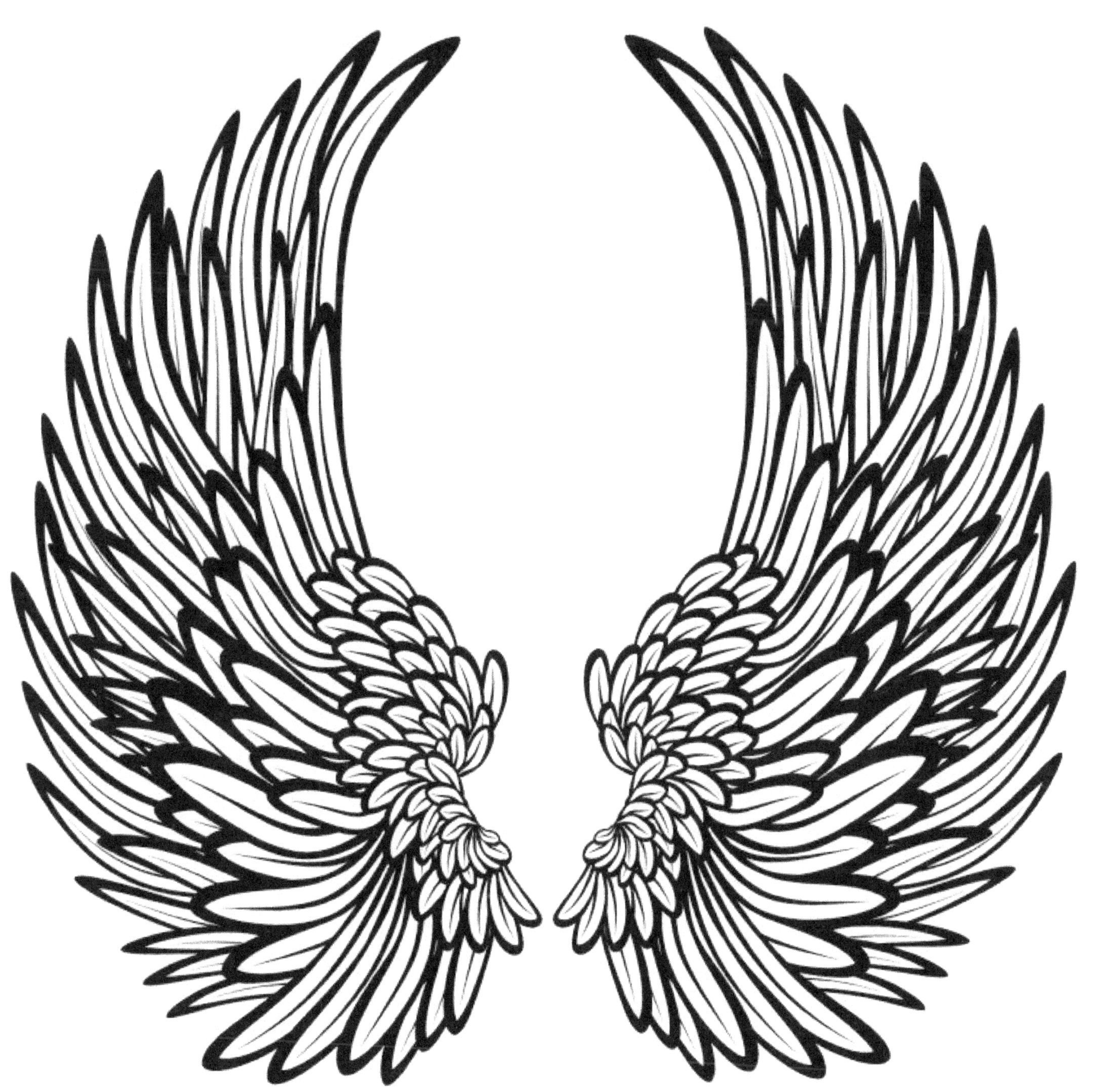

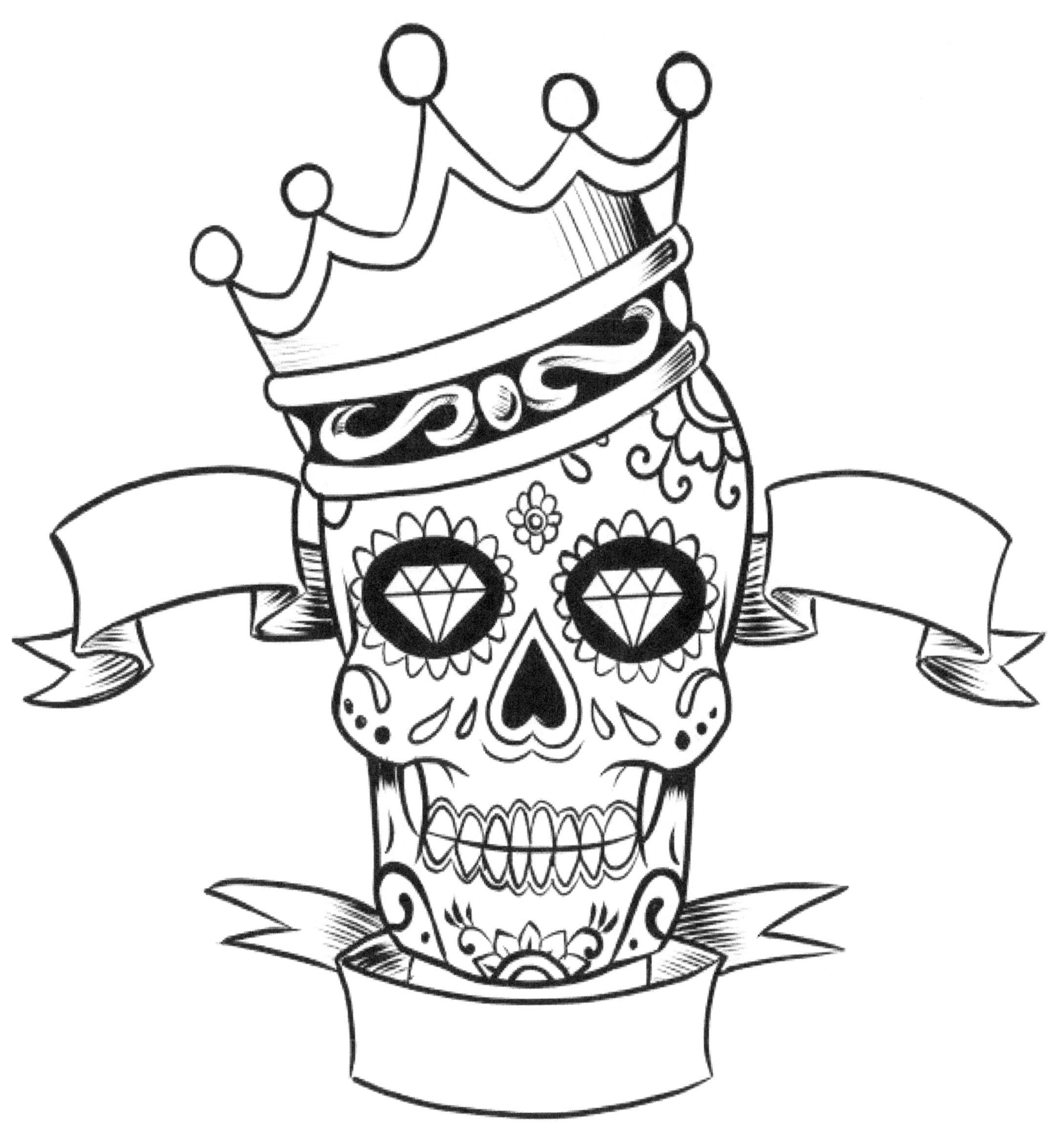

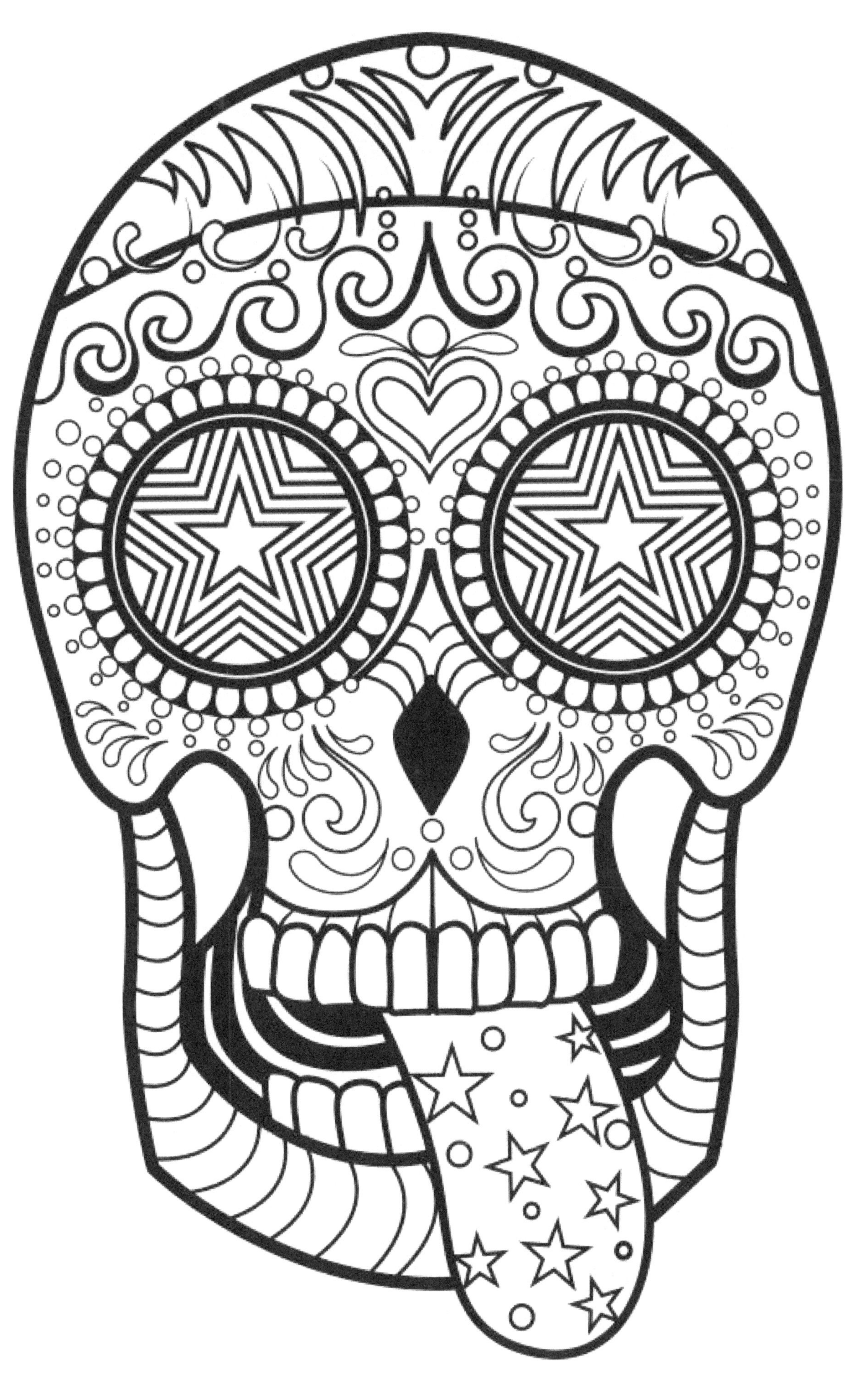

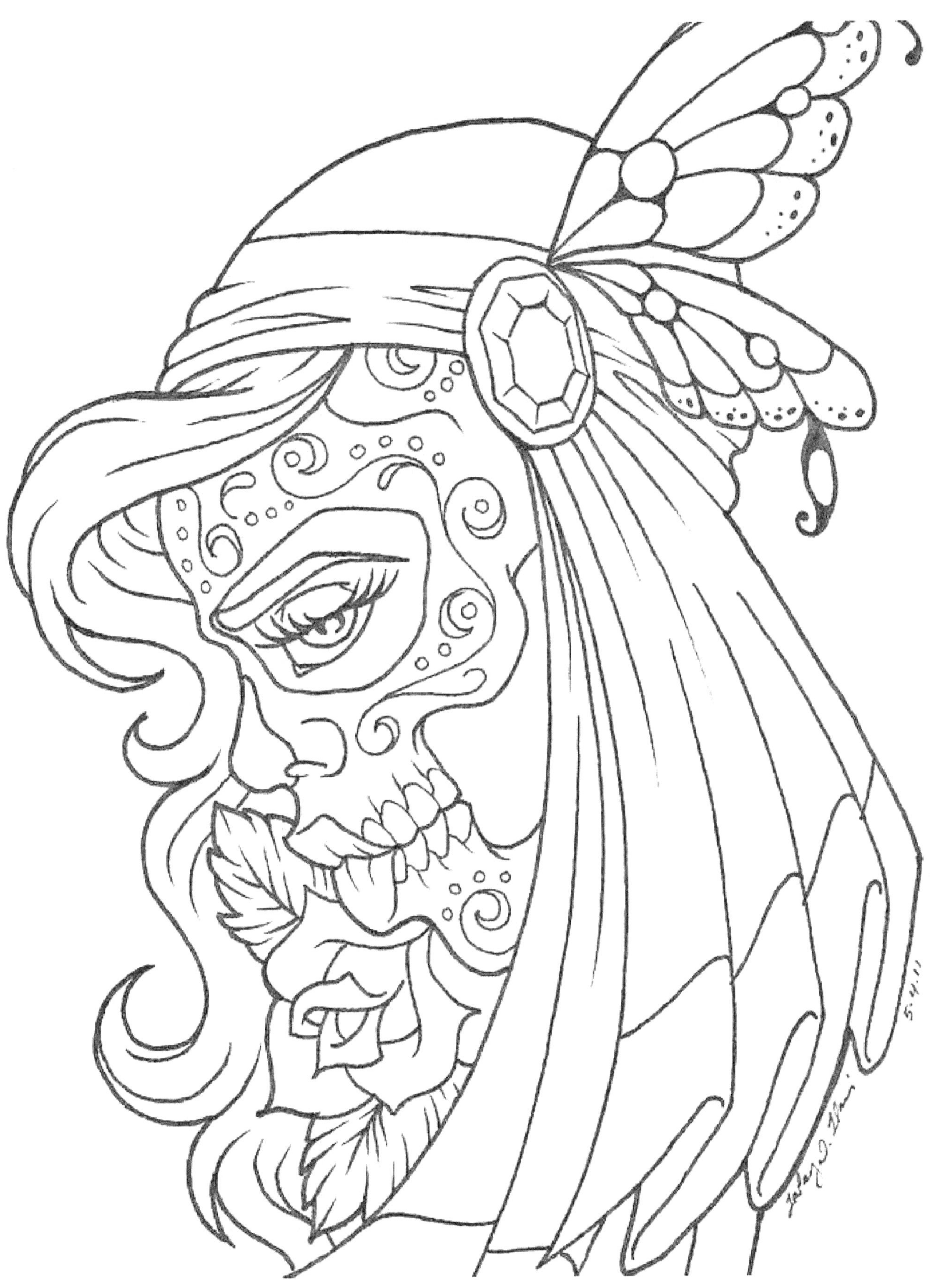

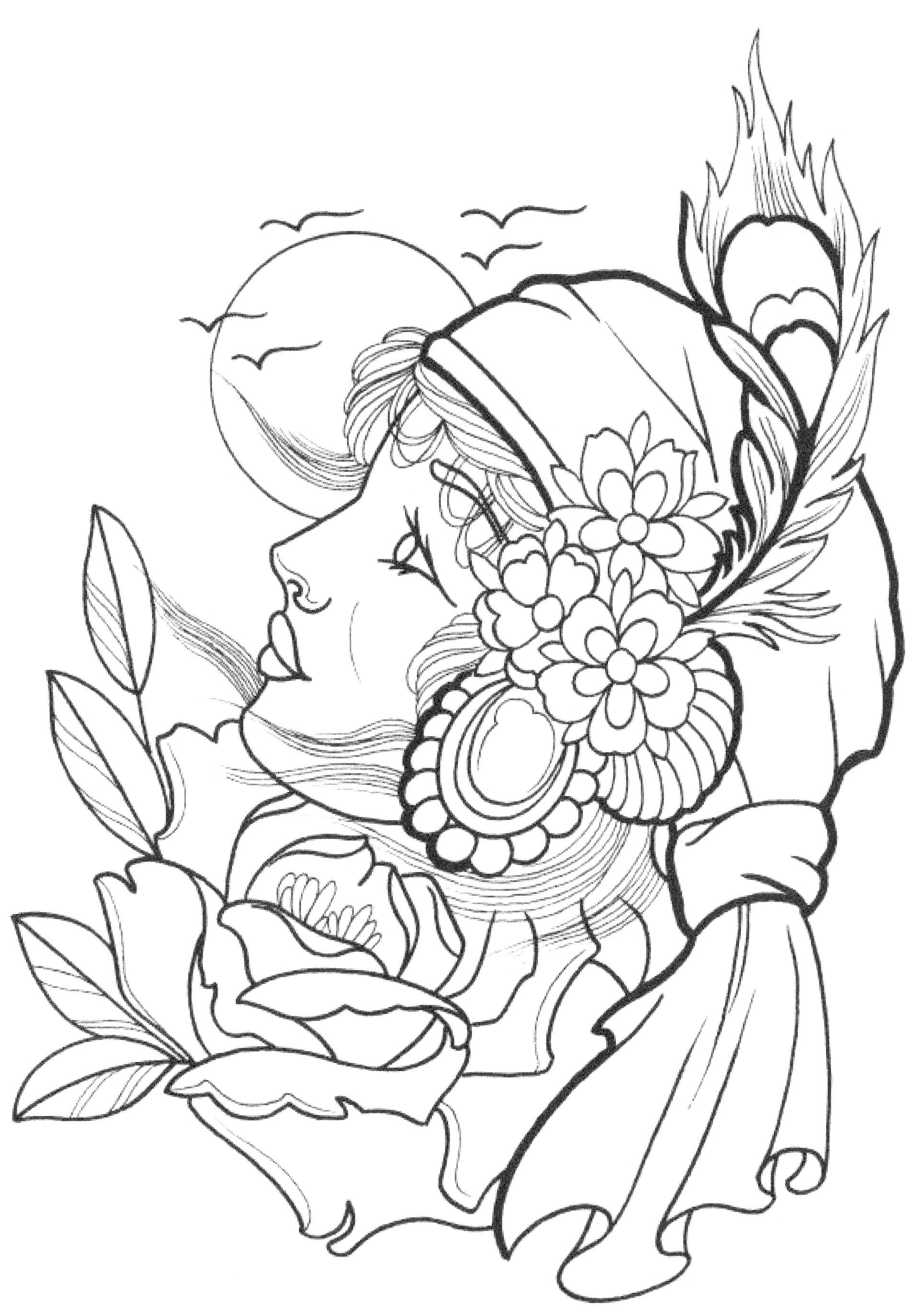

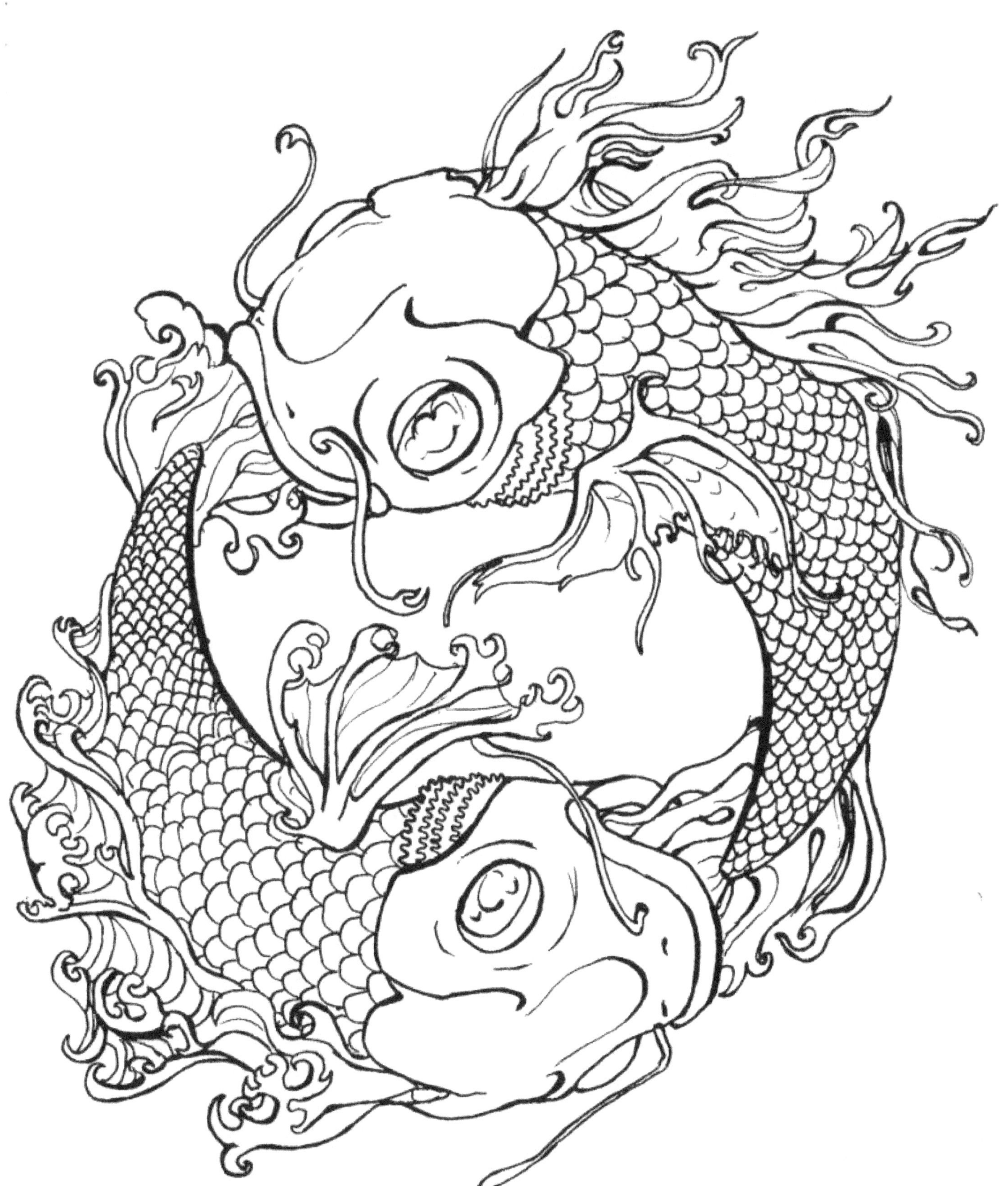